Technology and Justice

George Grant

Technology and Justice

Anansi / Toronto

Cover design: Katherine Adachi
Cover photograph of George Grant, courtesy of
    Dorothy Richardson.

Published with the assistance of the Canada Council and the Ontario Arts Council, and made in Canada for
House of Anansi Press Limited
35 Britain Street
Toronto, Ontario M5A 1R7

Canadian Cataloguing in Publication Data

Grant, George, 1918—
    Technology and justice

ISBN 0-88784-152-X

1. Technology—Moral and ethical aspects.
I. Title

BJ59.G73 1986   170   C86-094778-5

---

1 2   3   4   5   /   95   94   93   92   91   90   89   88   87   86

To R.S.G. and J.R.P.
sine quibus non

Contents

Preface

These writings centre around the modern paradigm of 'knowledge': behaviorist explanation in terms of algebra. This account is at the core of the fate of western civilisation. Because the conquest of human and non-human nature is at the heart of modern science, I describe that science as 'technological'.

In the first and second essays, I have tried to show why we should think of this account of knowledge as a fate and not something which in our freedom we can control. Because I continue to find it so difficult to understand this destiny, I have tried to think in terms of the Spanish proverb: "Take what you want, said God — take it and pay for it". This obviously applies not only to individuals but to civilisations.

In this book, I have tried to think what we have taken and how we have paid for the discovery of that paradigm of knowledge. Under payment, I have singled out how such a paradigm has shaped our thinking about justice — justice not only in the sense of this or that act, but in the sense of what we think justice itself to be. In the first two essays I deal with that question in a broadly theoretical way; in the last two, in terms of immediate practicality.

It will be the last two essays, I suspect, which will raise objections. In capitalist democracy, differences about practice are seen as important, while theoretical differences are seen as people's private business. It is of the very nature of 'technology' that this should be the case.

All that I write proceeds from sustained discussion with my wife. In that sense, she is the co-author of my writing and explicitly named such in the articles about euthanasia and abortion. Dennis Lee is a generous friend who gives of his precious time to help me to think and to write more clearly. Larry Schmidt has shown me much care and help over many years. Ann Wall and James Polk have taught me what a publisher should be. With their different souls, they combine to make being published a pleasure rather than a pain.

Some of these essays have appeared in quite different form elsewhere, and a list of acknowledgements with thanks is given at the back.

George Grant
August, 1986

Thinking About Technology

In each lived moment of our waking and sleeping, we are technological civilisation. Why is it best to characterise what we are encompassing, and are encompassed by, as technological? The answer can be seen in the very structure of the word. The current use of the word 'technology' in North America lays before us the particular novelty of our world.

In distinction from the usage in English of 'technology' and 'technologies', the Europeans have generally used 'technique' and 'techniques', the former for the whole array of means for making events happen, the latter for the particular means. They have claimed that our usage confuses us by distorting the literal meaning. The word 'technology' puts together the Greek word for 'art' and the word for the 'systematic study' of it, as the word 'biology' puts together 'bios' and 'logos'. They claim our usage parallels a similar imprecision in English in which 'history' means both the 'study' and 'what is studied'.

Nevertheless, although the European usage maintains verbal purity it does not evoke the modern reality as directly as ours. The very American neologism brings before us our novelty. When 'technology' is used to describe the actual means of making events happen, and not simply the systematic study of these means, the word reveals to us the fact that these new events happen because we westerners willed to develop a new and unique co-penetration of the arts and sciences, a co-penetration which has never before existed. What is given in the neologism—consciously or not—is the idea that modern civilisation is distinguished from all previous civilisations because our activities of knowing and making have been brought together in a way which does not allow the once-clear distinguishing of them. In fact, the coining of the word 'technology' catches the novelty of that co-penetration of knowing and making. It also implies that we have brought the sciences and the arts into a new unity in our will to be masters of the earth and beyond.

The use of the word 'technique' for that with which we have encompassed ourselves too easily leaves the implication that our understanding of what constitutes knowing and making is not radically different from that of previous civilisations. In fact, the modern 'technique' may seem at first to suggest the same kind of meaning as what is given in the Greek 'techne', as if we have simply progressed in efficiency of making. We then attribute our greater efficiency to the modern scientists, who guaranteed the progress of knowledge by clarifying its sure methods, and through that objective knowledge achieved greater ability to make things happen. In this account of progressing continuity, we assume that our modern western will to be the masters of the earth was taken for granted in the 'techne' of other civilisations. The time was not accidentally ripe; those peoples were not evolved enough to discover the sure path of science, which would have allowed them to realise that will to mastery.

With such implied 'histories' of the race, we close down on the startling novelty of the modern enterprise, and hide the difficulty of thinking it. We close down on the fact that modern technology is not simply an extension of human making through the power of a perfected science, but is a new account of what it is to know and to make in which both activities are changed by their co-penetration. We hide the difficulty of thinking that novelty, because in our implied 'histories' it is assumed that we can understand the novelty only from within its own account of knowing, which has itself become a kind of making.

Indeed the English word 'technology' with its Greek parts, and at the same time the novelty of what is given in their combination, shows what a transformation has taken place in our sciences, our arts and their interrelation, from what they were in our originating civilisation from which the parts of the word come. It is very difficult to grasp what is given about art and science in the Greek writings, because we understand previous sciences as preparations for our own, and other accounts of nature as stumbling provisions for our objective understanding of it. Nevertheless, at the simple surface of the question, it is clear that what was known in the physics of the Greeks was not knowledge of the kind that put the energies of nature at their disposal, as does modern western physics. It is only necessary to read Needham's history of Chinese science to see that the same was true there. What is given in Sanskrit shows this to be equally true of the civilisation founded upon the Vedanta.

When we speak of theoretical and applied science, the distinction contains something different from its ancient usage. 'Applied' means literally 'folded towards'. Einstein advised Roosevelt that in the light of the modern discoveries of physics, atomic weapons could be built, and that the Americans should organise to build them. Physics was being 'applied' not only in deciding that American interests-required the making of atomic weapons, but also in the sense that the very discoveries of the science were in their essence folded towards the mastery of the energies of nature, in a way that was absent in the pre-modern sciences. That co-penetration of knowing and making has quite changed what we mean by both the arts and the sciences from what was meant by them in the pre-modern era.

Why that foldedness towards potentialities of new makings has been implicit in modern science since its origins is extremely difficult to understand, and indeed has not yet been understood. That it has been so folded is expounded with consummate clarity in such writings as those of Bacon and Descartes, as they distinguished modern science from ancient science at the time of its very beginnings. The difficulty of understanding how and why it is so folded need not lead us to doubt that the folding is a fact. It is that fact which is given us in the neologism 'technology', and the novelty of that fact declares correct the characterisation of our society as technological. There may indeed be some other more perfect word to characterise our civilisation — some word which will come out of the understanding of what was being revealed when the European peoples brought forth those new sciences and arts. In the meantime, the word 'technological' catches best the uniqueness of our civilisation at its surface, and indicates the cause of its worldwide appeal.

In the novelties of our hourly existing, it is easy enough to recognise how much we have encompassed ourselves within technology. We sweep along super-highways to work in factories, or in the bureaucracy of some corporation; our needs are tended to in supermarkets and health complexes. We can cook, light, heat, refrigerate, be entertained at home through energy which has been produced and stored in quite new ways. If we have even a slight knowledge of the past we are aware that we can make happen what has never happened before, and we can have done to us what has never before been possible. At a higher level of attention we can recognise that our political and social decisions are interwoven with the pursuit and realisation of technological ends.

It is not suggested here that the technology with which we have surrounded ourselves is of only superficial or ambiguous benefit. Modern human beings since their beginnings have been moved by the faith that the mastery of nature would lead to the overcoming of hunger and labour, disease and war on so widespread a scale that at last we could build the world-wide society of free and equal people. One must never think about technological destiny without looking squarely at the justice in those hopes. Let none of us who live in the well-cushioned west speak with an aesthetic tiredness about our 'worldliness'.

Recently the more clear-sighted of our ruling classes have recognised that progress is a more complex matter than was envisaged by those who had believed that a better society would arise ineluctably from technology. In the past human beings have been responsible for the destruction of all the members of some other species; but today when we watch the osprey's glory in the ocean storm, there is not only awareness that this beauty may be passing away, because the eggs of the bird are being sterilised by our use of chemicals, but also that the source of life itself may become no longer a home of life. Our novelty lies in the fact that where Plato warned clearly against the dirtying of the waters, he did not face their pollution as a possibility in

the immediate future. We are now faced with easily cal-
culable crises (concerning population resources, pollution,
etc.) which have been consequent upon the very drive to
mastery itself. The political response to these interlocking
emergencies has been a call for an even greater mobilisation of technology, which illustrates the determining power
of our technological representation of reality. More technology is needed to meet the emergencies which technology has produced.

Much of the new technology upon which we are going to
depend to meet these crises in the 'developed' world is
technology turned towards human beings. The new adage
of rulers and educators is that to the mastery of non-human
nature must now be added mastery of ourselves. The desire
for 'mastery of ourselves' (which generally means the
mastery of other people) results in the proliferation of new
arts and sciences directed towards human control, so that
we can be shaped to live consonantly with the demands of
mass society. These can be seen applied through the com-
puterised bureaucracies of the private and public corporations, through mass education, medicine and the media
etc. Many scientists are now, above all, planners and central
members of the ruling class. The proliferating power of the
medical profession illustrates our drive to new technologies of human nature. This expanding power has gen -
erally been developed by people concerned with human
betterment.

Yet nonetheless, the profession has become a chief
instrument for tightening social control in the western
world, as is made evident by the unity of the profession's
purpose with those of political administration and law
enforcement, the complex organisation of dependent professions it has gathered around itself, its taking over of the
cure of the 'psyche', and the increasing correlation of psy-

chiatry with a behaviourally and physiologically oriented psychology. It becomes increasingly necessary to adjust the masses to behave appropriately amidst such technological crises as those of population and pollution and life in the cities.

The thinker who has most deeply pondered our technological destiny has stated that the new co-penetrated arts and sciences are now proceeding to the apogee of their determining power around the science of cybernetics. The science of the steersman comes to be present in all other sciences. Heidegger's proposition does not mean anything as ill-thought as the statement, common a few years ago, that natural sciences and engineering are becoming dependent on the social sciences. That statement is shown to be silly by the dependence of all the social sciences (in so far as they are attempting to be modern sciences and not simply covert moralities or ideologies or a mixture of both) upon biochemistry, and of biochemistry upon physics. To put simply what is meant: the mobilisation of the objective arts and sciences at their apogee comes more and more to be unified around the planning and control of human activity. What must be emphasised here is that the new technologies of both human and non-human nature have been the dominant responses to the crises caused by technology itself. This illustrates how 'technology' is the pervasive mode of being in our political and social lives.

The name 'technological' may indeed be a word too much on the surface for the best articulation of what is being lived and thought in the western ways which are becoming world wide. Is there some primal affirmation which is 'before' technology—that is, before our science and techniques, before our political and social ways, before our philosophies and theologies? When the 'before' in that sentence is thought chronologically (or, as we like to say, historically), was there some originating affirmation made somewhere and sometime when Europeans defined themselves over against the classical civilisation they were inheriting? Many scholars have written of the details of the arts and sciences, the struggles and reverences of that originating time; some philosophers have attempted to bring such a self-definition into the light of day. But who has succeeded in laying before us in a convincing unity what it was that gave the Europeans their special destiny, what primal affirmation penetrated their life and thought? Without denial of the unfathomedness of this affirmation, I would be willing to say that Europeans somehow seem to have come to an apprehension of the whole as 'will'. That apprehension came to them as they tried to relate what had been given in ancient philosophy to the exclusivity which they had taken from the Bible. Yet such an attempt to understand what is 'before' technology leaves one only with dim and uncertain language. As one turns back to the surface, it is adequate to call our society 'technological', because its dominant manifestation is the new co-penetrated arts and sciences.

The novelties of that destiny lie before us in every lived moment. However, what exactly constitutes the noveleness of these novelties is more difficult to apprehend. How novel are these novelties? When we speak of technology as a new set of occurrences in the world, what do we mean by newness in that context? What constitutes the particular newness or novelness of technology, and what is newness or novelty itself? If following the English dictionary we speak of the new as the strange and unfamiliar, how strange and unfamiliar is our technological society? What do we mean by strangeness and unfamiliarity, and how do we ever apprehend it? To descend to the practical, if we are able to apprehend correctly the particular novelty of our technological society, what does it portend for the future?

Most of us represent that novelty to ourselves as a great step forward in the systematic application of reason to the invention of instruments for our disposal. Human beings have from their beginnings developed instruments to help them get things done (indeed in our era many distinguish human beings from the other animals by calling us the tool-making animals). The word 'instrument' is not confined simply to external objects such as machines or drugs or hydro power, but includes such development of systems of organisation and communication as bureaucracies and factories. Technology is then thought of as the whole apparatus of instruments made by man and placed at the disposal of man for his choice and purposes. In this account, the novelness lies in the fact that in our civilisation the activity of inventing instruments reaches new levels of effectiveness because it has been systematically related to our science, and our science has at last discovered the sure path of a methodology which has allowed it progress in objective discovery.

This representation of technology as an array of instruments, lying at the free disposal of the species which creates them, seems so obviously true as to be beyond argument. Nevertheless this account of technology as instrument, however undeniable, tends to pare down the actual novelness of our situation, so that we are not allowed to contemplate that situation for what it is.

For example, a computer scientist recently made the following statement about the machines he helps to invent: "The computer does not impose on us the ways it should be used". Obviously the statement is made by someone who is aware that computers can be used for purposes of which he does not approve—for example, the tyrannous control of human beings. This is given in the word 'should'. He makes a statement in terms of his intimate knowledge of computers which transcends that intimacy, in that it is more than a description of any given computer or of what is technically common to all such machines. Because he wishes to state something about the possible good or evil purposes for which computers can be used, he expresses, albeit in negative form, what computers are, in a way which is more than their technical description. They are instruments, made by human skill for the purpose of achieving certain human goals. They are neutral instruments in the sense that the morality of the goals for which they are used is determined outside them.

Many people who have never seen a computer, and only slightly understand the capacity of computers, have the sense from their daily life that they are being managed by them, and have perhaps an undifferentiated fear about the potential extent of this management. This man, who knows about the invention and use of these machines, states what they are in order to put our sense of anxiety into a perspective freed from the terrors of such fantasies as the myth of Doctor Frankenstein. His perspective assumes that the machines are instruments, because their capacities have been built into them by human beings, and it is human beings who operate those machines for purposes they have determined. All instruments can obviously be used for bad purposes, and the more complex the capacities of the instrument, the more complex can be its possible bad uses. But if we apprehend these machines for what they are, neutral instruments which we in our freedom are called upon to control, we are better able to come to terms rationally with their potential dangers. The first step in coping with these dangers is to see that they are related to the potential decisions of human beings about how to use computers, not to the inherent capacities of the machines themselves. Indeed the statement about the computer gives the prevalent 'liberal' view of the modern situation which is so rooted in us that it seems to be common sense itself, even rationality itself. We have certain technological capacities; it is up to us to use those capacities for decent human purposes.

Yet despite the seeming common sense of the statement, when we try to think the sentence "the computer does not impose on us the ways it should be used," it becomes clear that we are not allowing computers to appear before us for what they are. Indeed the statement (like many similar) obscures for us what computers are. To begin at the surface: the words "the computer does not impose" are concerned with the capacities of these machines, and these capacities are brought before us as if they existed in abstraction from the events which have made possible their existence. Obviously the machines have been made from a vast variety of materials, consummately fashioned by a vast apparatus of fashioners. Their existence has required generations of sustained effort by chemists, metallurgists and workers in mines and factories. Beyond these obvious facts, computers have been made within the new science and its mathematics. That science is a particular paradigm of knowledge and, as any paradigm of knowledge, is to be understood as the relation between an aspiration of human thought and the effective conditions for its realisation.

It is not my purpose here to describe that paradigm in detail; nor would it be within my ability to show its interrelation with mathematics conceived as algebra. Suffice it to say that what is given in the modern use of the word 'science' is the project of reason to gain 'objective' knowledge. And modern 'reason' is the summoning of anything before a subject and putting it to the question, so that it gives us its reasons for being the way it is as an object. A paradigm of knowledge is not something reserved for scientists and scholars. Anybody who is awake in any part of our educational system knows that this paradigm of knowledge stamps the institutions of that system, their curricula, in their very heart, in what the young are required to know and to be able to do if they are to be called 'qualified'. That paradigm of knowledge is central to our civilisational destiny and has made possible the existence of computers. I mean by 'civilisational destiny' above all the fundamental presuppositions that the majority of human beings inherit in a civilisation, and which are so taken for granted as the way things are that they are given an almost absolute status. To describe a destiny is not to judge it. It may indeed be, as many believe, that the development of that paradigm is a great step in the ascent of man, that it is the essence of human liberation, even that its development justifies the human experiment itself. Whatever the truth of these beliefs, the only point here is that without this destiny computers would not exist. And like all destinies, they 'impose'.

What has been said about the computer's existence depending upon the paradigm of knowlege is of course equally true of the earlier machines of industrialism. The western paradigm of knowledge has not been static, but has been realised in a dynamic unfolding, and one aspect of that realisation has been a great extension of what is given in the conception of 'machine'. We all know that computers are machines for the transmitting of information, not the transformation of energy. They require software as well as hardware. They have required the development of mathematics as algebra, and of algebra as almost identical with logic. Their existence has required a fuller realisation of the western paradigm of knowledge beyond its origins, in this context the extension of the conception of machine. It may well be said that where the steel press may be taken as the image of Newtonian physics and mathematics, the computer can be taken as the image of contemporary physics and mathematics. Yet in making that distinction, it must also be said that contemporary science and Newtonian science are equally moments in the realisation of the same paradigm.

The phrase "the computer does not impose" misleads, because it abstracts the computer from the destiny that was required for its making. Common sense may tell us that the computer is an instrument, but it is an instrument from within the destiny which *does* 'impose' itself upon us, and therefore the computer *does* impose.

To go further: How are we being asked to take the word 'ways' in the assertion that 'the computer does not impose the ways'? Even if the purposes for which the computer's capacities should be used are determined outside itself, do not these capacities limit the kind of ways for which it can be used? To take a simple example from the modern institutions of learning and training: in most jurisdictions there are cards on which children are assessed as to their 'skills' and 'behaviour', and this information is retained by computers. It may be granted that such information adds little to the homogenising vision inculcated throughout society by such means as centrally controlled curricula or teacher training. It may also be granted that as computers and their programming become more sophisticated the information stored therein may be able to take more account of differences. Nevertheless, it is clear that the ways that computers can be used for storing and transmitting information can only be ways that increase the tempo of the homogenising processes. Abstracting facts so that they can be stored as information is achieved by classification, and it is the very nature of any classifying to homogenise. Where classification rules, identities and differences can appear only in its terms. Indeed the word 'information' is itself perfectly attuned to the account of knowledge which is homogenising in its very nature. 'Information' is about objects, and comes forth as part of that science which summons objects to give us their reasons.

It is not my purpose at this point to discuss the complex issues of good and evil involved in the modern movement towards homgeneity, nor to discuss the good of heterogeneity, which in its most profound past form was an expression of autochthony. Some modern thinkers state that beyond the rootlessness characteristic of the present early stages of technological society, human beings are now called to new ways of being rooted which will have passed through modern rootlessness, and will be able at one and the same time to accept the benefits of modern homogenisation while living out a new form of heterogeneity. These statements are not at issue here. Rather my purpose is to point out that the sentence about computers hides the fact that their ways are always homogenising. Because this is hidden, questioning homogenisation is closed down in the sentence.

To illustrate the matter from another aspect of technological development: Canadians wanted the most efficient car for geographic circumstances and social purposes similar to those of the people who first developed the mass-produced automobile. Our desire for and use of such cars has been a central cause of our political and economic integration and our social homogenisation with the people of the imperial heartland. This was not only because of the vast corporate structures necessary for building and keeping in motion such automobiles, and the direct and indirect political power of such corporations, but also because any society with such vehicles tends to become like any other society with the same. Seventy-five years ago somebody might have said "The automobile does not impose on us the ways it should be used", and who would have quarrelled with that? Yet this would have been a deluded representation of the automobile.

Obviously, human beings may still be able to control, by strict administrative measures, the ways that cars are used. They may prevent the pollution of the atmosphere or prevent freeways from destroying central city life. It is to be hoped that cities such as Toronto will maintain themselves as communities by winning popular victories over expressways and airports. Whatever efforts may be made, they will not allow us to represent the automobile to ourselves as a neutral instrument.

Obviously the 'ways' that automobiles and computers can be used are dependent on their being investment-heavy machines which require large institutions for their production. The potential size of such corporations can be imagined in the statement of a reliable economist: if the present growth of I.B.M. is extrapolated, that corporation will in the next thirty years be a larger unit than the economy of any presently constituted national state, including that of its homeland. At the simplest factual level, computers can be built only in societies in which there are large corporations. This will be the case whatever ways these institutions are related to the states in which they are incorporated, be that relation some form of capitalism or some form of socialism. Also those machines have been and will continue to be instruments with effect beyond the confines of particular nation states. They will be the instruments of the imperialism of certain communities towards other communities. They are instruments in the struggle between competing empires, as the present desire of the Soviet Union for American computers illustrates. It might be that "in the long run of progress", humanity will come to the universal and homogeneous state in which individual empires and nations have disappeared. That in itself would be an even larger corporation. To express the obvious: whatever conceivable political and economic alternatives there may be, computers can only exist in societies in which there are large corporate institutions. The ways they can be used are limited to those situations. In this sense computers are not neutral instruments, but instruments which exclude certain forms of community and permit others.

In our era, many believe that the great question about technology is whether the ways it is used will be determined by the standards of justice in one or other of the dominant political philosophies. The rationalism of the west has produced not only modern physical science, but also modern political philosophy. Technology is considered neutral, and its just use will depend upon the victory of true rather than false political philosophy. The appeal of the teachings of political philosophers has been massive in our era, because these teachings have taken the form of ideologies which convince the minds of masses of human beings. The ways that computers should be used can be solved satisfactorily if political regimes are shaped by the true philosophy. The three dominant alternatives are capitalist liberalism, communist Marxism, and national socialist historicism.

What calls out for recognition here is that the same account of reason which produced the technologies also produced the accounts of justice given in these modern political philosophies. It led, moreover, to the public manifestation of those political philosophies as ideologies. The statement "the computer does not impose on us the ways it should be used" abstracts from the fact that "the ways" that the computer will be used will be determined by politics in the broadest sense of that term. Politics in our era are dominated by accounts of society which came forth from the same account of reasoning that produced the new co-penetrated arts and sciences.

It cannot be my purpose at this point to show the nature of that sameness. Such a demonstration would require a detailed history of the modern west. It would require above all a demonstration of the mutual interdependence of the modern physical sciences and the modern moral sciences as they were both defined against the account of science in classical philosophy. Much of the enormous enterprise of modern scholarship has been taken up with the detailed mapping of what was done and thought and made by large numbers of inventors, scientists, artists, philosophers, politicians, religious reformers etc. Beyond scholarship, the demonstration of this interdependence would require the ability to think what was being thought by the greatest scientists and philosophers. By distinguishing the new science from the account of science in the ancient world they laid down the modern affirmations concerning what is. Concerning the conception of justice, it would be necessary to follow how great philosophers such as Descartes and Locke, Rousseau and Nietzsche, understood the unity between the findings of modern science and their accounts of justice.

Without attempting any of these demonstrations, suffice it to state that the ways that computers have been and will be used cannot be detached from modern conceptions of justice, and that these conceptions of justice come forth from the very account of reasoning which led to the building of computers. This is not to say anything here concerning the truth or falsity of modern conceptions of justice, nor is it to prejudge the computer by some reactionary account stemming from the desire to turn one's back on the modern. It is simply to assert that we are not in the position where computers lie before us as neutral instruments, and where we use them according to standards of justice which are reached outside of the existence of the computers themselves. The instruments and the standards of justice are bound together, both belonging to the same destiny of modern reason. The failure to recognize this hides from us the truth about the 'ways' computers can be used.

The force of that destiny is to be seen, finally, in the ambiguity of the word 'should' in the statement, "The computer does not impose on us the ways it should be used". Our novel situation is presented as if human beings 'should' use computers for certain purposes and not for others. But what has the word 'should' come to mean in advanced technological societies?

'Should' was originally the past tense of 'shall'. It is still sometimes used in a conditional sense to express greater uncertainty about the future than the prophetic sense of 'shall'. ('I shall get a raise this year' is more certain than 'I should get a raise this year'. The colloquialism from the home of our language, 'I shouldn't wonder,' expresses this.) In its origins, 'shall' was concerned with 'owing', when used as a transitive verb. Chaucer wrote: "And by that feyth I shal to god and yow". But over the centuries 'should' took over from 'shall' as the word with the connotation of owing, and could be used for that purpose intransitively.

The sentence "The computer does not impose on us the ways it should be used" is concerned with human actions which are owed. If the statement were in positive form — "The computer does impose on us the ways it should be used" — the debt would probably be understood as owed by human beings to machines. We can say of a good car that we owe it to the car to lubricate it properly. We would mean it in the same sense if we were to say we owe it to ourselves to try not to contradict ourselves, if we wish to think out some matter clearly. If we want the car to do what it is fitted for—which is, in traditional usage, its good—then we must look after it. But the 'should' in the statement about the computer is clearly not being used about what is owed by men to machines. The sentence is concerned with the just use of the machine as instrument. 'Should' expresses that we ought to use it justly. But what is the nature of the debt there spoken? To what or to whom do we owe it? Is that debt conditional? For example, if human beings 'should' use computers only in ways that are compatible with constitutional government, and not to promote tyranny, to what or to whom is this support of constitutional government owed? To ourselves? to other human beings? all, or some of them? to nature? to history? to reasonableness? to God?

Because of the ambiguity which has fallen upon all accounts of owing, our era has often been described as a time of nihilism. As many Europeans came to believe over the last three hundred years that their affirmations about goodness could not find foundations in accounts of God or nature, reason or history, the result for many has been a state of mind which is well described as nihilism. This state of mind has had wide public influence because the mass literacy necessary to technological society made nihilism a situation open not only to the few. In North America the organisation of training in schools and multiversities has produced mass 'wised-upness', which is the democratic edition of nihilism.

Nevertheless it is necessary to be careful at this point. Characterising technological society as essentially nihilistic prejudges the whole question of what it is. Such a dismayed reaction is as likely to close down thought about its nature as much as does any progressivism. If we use the word 'good' in the simplest way as what we approve, and 'bad' as what we deplore, is it not evident that large major-ities now give their shared approval to certain activities and that from those activites we can apprehend a positive modern conception of goodness? For example, is it not generally believed that freedom for sexual realisation in its varying particularities should be promoted in societies? Or, if one has any knowledge of the modern scientific community, is one not aware of the positive expectations about its accomplishments which permeate that commu-nity, from which a positive conception of goodness can be deduced?

A description of the modern era fairer than that of nihil-ism is that a great change has taken place in the public conceiving of goodness. The enunciation of that change is best made in terms of what is positive in both the past and the prevalently modern accounts. The originating western conception of goodness is of that which meets us with the overriding claim of justice, and persuades us that in desir-ing obedience to that claim we will find what we are fitted for. The modern conception of goodness is of our free creating of richness and greatness of life and all that is advantageous thereto. The presently popular phrase in the modern account is 'quality of life'.

The modern conception of goodness does not include the assertion of a claim upon us which properly orders our desires in terms of owing, and which is itself the route and fulfilment for desire. In the prevalent modern view, owing is always provisional upon what we desire to create. Obviously we live in the presence of the existence of others, and our creating may perforce be limited because of what is currently permitted legally to be done to others. However the limitations put upon creating by the claims of others, whether nationally or internationally, are understood as contractual: that is, provisional. This exclusion of nonprovisory owing from our interpretation of desire means that what is summoned up by the word 'should' is no longer what was summoned up among our ancestors. What moderns hear always includes an 'if': it is never "beyond all bargains and without an alternative". Moreover, the arrival in the world of this changed interpretation of goodness is interrelated to the arrival of technological civilisation. The liberation of human desiring from any supposed excluding claim, so that it is believed we freely create values, is a face of the same liberation in which men overcame chance by technology—the liberty to make happen what we want to make happen. We are free, not only in what we want to make happen, but also in choosing the means. The whole of nature becomes more and more at our disposal as if it were nothing in itself but only our 'raw material'.

"The computer does not impose on us the ways it *should* be used" asserts the essence of the modern view, which is that human ability freely determines what happens. It then puts that freedom in the service of the very 'should' which that same modern novelty has made provisional. The resolute mastery to which we are summoned in 'does not impose' is the very source of difficulty in apprehending goodness as 'should'. Therefore, the 'should' in the statement has only a masquerading resonance in the actions we are summoned to concerning computers. It is a word carried over from the past to be used in a present which is ours only because the assumptions of that past were criticised out of public existence. The statement therefore cushions us from the full impact of the novelties it asks us to consider. It pads us against wondering about the disappearance of 'should' in its ancient resonance, and what this disappearance may portend for the future.

I have written at length about this statement to illustrate how difficult it is to apprehend correctly the novelness of our novelties. When we represent technology to ourselves as an array of neutral instruments, invented by human beings and under human control, we are expressing a kind of common sense, but it is a common sense from within the very technology we are attempting to represent. The novelness of our novelties is being minimized. We are led to forget that the modern destiny permeates our representations of the world and ourselves. The coming to be of technology has required changes in what we think is good, what we think good is, how we conceive sanity and madness, justice and injustice, rationality and irrationality, beauty and ugliness.

Indeed there is novelty in how we now conceive novelness itself. That changed conception of novelness also obviously entails a change in the traditional account of an openness to the whole, and therefore a quite new content to the word 'philosophy'. A road or a sparrow, a child or the passing of time come to us through that destiny. To put the matter crudely: when we represent technology to ourselves through its own common sense we think of ourselves as picking and choosing in a supermarket, rather than within the analogy of the package deal. We have bought a package deal of far more fundamental novelty than simply a set of instruments under our control. It is a destiny which enfolds us in its own conceptions of instrumentality, neutrality and purposiveness. It is in this sense that it has been truthfully said: technology is the ontology of the age. Western peoples (and perhaps soon all peoples) take themselves as subjects confronting otherness as objects—objects lying as raw material at the disposal of knowing and making subjects. Unless we comprehend the package deal we obscure from ourselves the central difficulty in our present destiny: we apprehend our destiny by forms of thought which are themselves the very core of that destiny.

The result of this is that when we are deliberating in any practical situation our judgement acts rather like a mirror, which throws back the very metaphysic of the technology which we are supposed to be deliberating about in detail. The outcome is almost inevitably a decision for further technological development. For example, we can see this in the recent public discussions concerning research into the recombinations made possible by the discovery of the structure of DNA. The victory of those espousing the development of such research was not based simply on the power of the community of scientists to guarantee their freedom under the banner of Robert Oppenheimer's *bon mot* about experiment: "when you see something that is technically sweet, you go ahead and do it." It was rather that those (both inside and outside the scientific community) who were troubled about the possibilities in such research could not pass beyond the language of immediate dangers in expressing their concern. Once the scientists showed how the immediate threats could be met, the case was closed. The opponents of the research could not pass beyond the language of specifiable dangers, because any possible long range intimations of deprival of human good could not be expressed in the ontology they shared with their opponents. The ontology expressed in such terms as 'the ascent of life', 'human beings making their own future', 'the progress of knowledge', or 'the necessity of interfering with nature for human good' could not be used against itself. But there is no other language available which does not seem to be the irrational refusal of the truths of scientific discovery.

Any deliberate 'no' to particular researches requires thinking the truth of the distinction made in the old adage *a posse ad esse non valet consequentia.* (I take this to mean: just because something can be, it does not follow that it should be.) But the account of existence which arises from the modern co-penetration of knowing and making exalts the possible above what is. It has undermined our ability to think that there could be knowledge of what is in terms of which the justice of every possible action could be judged in advance of any possible future. It is not feasible here (and who indeed is capable of that task?) to spell out in detail how in and through modern science and philosophy, or even in and through the poor remnants of theology (which may be called German theology), the possible is exalted above what is. However, the matter can be put simply: if we hold in our minds the two statements, *A posse ad esse non valet consequentia* and "When you see something that is technically sweet you go ahead and do it", and when you argue about what to do about it only after you have had your technical success— then is there any doubt which statement is congruent with the sense of our own creativity as knowers and makers?

Consequently, for those who affirm that the justice or injustice of some actions can be known in advance of the necessities of time and of the calculation of means, there is a pressing need to understand our technological destiny from principles more comprehensive than its own. This need lifts us up to ask about the great western experiment in a more than piecemeal way. It pushes us to try to understand its meaning in terms of some openness to the whole which is not simply sustenance for the further realisation of that experiment. But the exigency of our need for understanding must not blind us to the tightening circle in which we find ourselves. We are called to understand technological civilisation just when its very realisation has radically put in question the possibility that there could be any such understanding.

Faith and the Multiversity

"Don't let me catch anyone talking about the Universe in my department!" — Lord Rutherford

I

"Faith and the multiversity" is a subject which could be tackled from many angles, both practical and theoretical. The essence of the issues is, however, the relation between faith and modern science. It might be maintained that there has already been enough discussion of this over the last centuries. I do not agree. Thought has not yet reached the core of that relation. Many Christians turn away from the relation because they want there to be no conflict here. Nevertheless it remains fate-filled with conflict.

It is important to be clear what is meant by the multiversity, particularly because it is an institution which has realised itself in Europe and North America only in the last half of this century—although its coming to be was a slow emergence over the last four centuries. I often meet

people of my generation who went to university in the
1930s, and who speak as if the institutions their children or
grandchildren are now attending are really the same as
those they went to. But this is simply an illusion. The
names are the same, but they are such different places that
they should have different names. To say what they now
are, it is necessary to describe the dominating paradigm of
knowledge which rules them and determines what they are.

Different civilisations have different paradigms of knowledge, and such paradigms shape every part of the society.
The principle of any paradigm in any civilisation is always
the relation between an aspiration of human thought and
the effective conditions for its validation.

The question then becomes what is given in the modern
use of the word 'science'. This is the paradigm which has
slowly reached definition over the last centuries, and has
since 1945 come to its apogee of determining power over
our institutions. Of course, it would be folly to attempt to
summarise in a paragraph the results of that brilliant progress of self-definition by philosophic scientists.

Suffice it simply to say that what is given in the modern
paradigm is the project of reason to gain objective knowledge. What is meant by objective? Object means literally
some thing that we have thrown over against ourselves. *Jacio*
I throw, *ob* over against; therefore "the thrown against". The
German word for object is *Gegenstand*—that which stands
against. Reason as project, (that is, reason as thrown forth)
is the summonsing of something before us and the putting
of questions to it, so that it is forced to give its reasons for
being the way it is as an object. Our paradigm is that we
have knowledge when we represent anything to ourselves
as object, and question it, so that it will give us its reasons.
That summonsing and questioning requires well-defined
procedures. These procedures are what we call in English

'experimental research', although what is entailed in these is more clearly given in the German word *Forschung*. Often people in the university like to use about themselves the more traditional word 'scholar', but that word means now those who carry on 'research'. Those procedures started with such experiments as balls running down an inclined plane, but now the project of reason applies them to everything: stones, plants, human and non-human animals. Thus in North America we have divided our institutions of higher learning into faculties of natural science, social science and humanities, depending on the object which is being researched. But the project of reason is largely the same, to summons different things to questioning.

In the case of the humanities the object is the past, and these procedures are applied to the relics of the past. For example, I have lived in a department of religion in which much work was done to summons the Bible before the researchers to give them its reasons. Each department of these institutions, indeed almost each individual researcher, carries on the project of reason by approaching different objects. The limitations of the human mind in synthesising facts necessitates the growing division of research into differing departments and further subdivisions. This paradigm of knowledge makes it therefore appropriate to speak of the multiversity.

The achievements of the modern project are of course a source of wonder. The world as object has indeed given forth its reasons, as it has been summonsed to do over the last centuries. The necessities that we now can know about stones or societies surely produce in us astonishment. These achievements are not simply practical, but also have theoretical consequences. All of us in our everyday lives are so taken up with certain practical achievements, in medicine, in production, in the making of human beings and the making of war, that we are apt to forget the sheer theoretical interest of what has been revealed about necessity in modern physics or biology.

My purpose is to discuss the relation of this paradigm of knowledge to faith. 'Faith' is one of the central words of western thought which has had many meanings. What I intend by it is Simone Weil's definition: "Faith is the experience that the intelligence is enlightened by love."[1] Such a sentence, of course, simply moves one from the uncertainty of 'faith' to the even greater complexity of the word 'love'. Obviously this word has been used to cover a multitude of disparate meanings. Heidegger has used the beautiful metaphor that language is the house of being. In our epigonal times that house has become a labyrinth. Nowhere are we more in that labyrinth than when we try to sort out the relation between such words as 'love', 'desire', and 'appetite' etc. I cannot attempt that sorting out here, but will simply express what I think is given in the word 'love' in the sentence about faith.[2]

What is first intended is that love is consent to the fact that there is authentic otherness. We all start with needs, and with dependence on others to meet them. As we grow up, self-consciousness brings the tendency to make ourselves the centre, and with it the commonsense understanding that the very needs of survival depend on our own efforts. These facts push us in the direction of egocentricity. When life becomes dominated by self-serving, the reality of otherness, in its own being, almost disappears for us. In sexual life, where most of us make some contact with otherness, there is yet a tendency to lose sight of it, so that we go on wanting things from others just as we fail to recognize their authentic otherness. In all the vast permutations and combinations of sexual desire the beauty of otherness is both present and absent. Indeed, the present tendency for sexual life and family to be held apart is frightening, because for most people children have been the means whereby they were presented with unequivocal otherness. In political terms, Plato places the tyrant as the worst human being because his self-serving has gone to the farthest point. He is saying that the tyrant is mad because otherness has ceased to exist for him. I can grasp with direct recognition the theological formulation of this: "Hell is to be one's own."[3]

The old teaching was that we love otherness, not because it is other, but because it is beautiful. The beauty of others was believed to be an experience open to everyone, though in extraordinarily different forms, and at differing steps towards perfection. It was obviously capable of being turned into strange channels because of the vicissitudes of our existence. The shoe fetishist, the farmer and St. John of the Cross were on the same journey, but at different stages. The beauty of otherness is the central assumption in the statement, "Faith is the experience that the intelligence is enlightened by love."

Nevertheless, any statement about the beauty of the world is so easily doubted in our era, because it appears meaningless within the dominant language of modern science. Our uses of 'beauty' have been radically subjectivised. "Beauty is in the eye of the beholder." (But what then is beholding?) At the simplest level it is said that the sentence, "We love otherness because it is beautiful," is tautologous, because beauty is already defined as what we love. Our loves are determined by the vast varieties of necessities and chances which have constituted our desires, and these could 'ideally' be explained by behavioural psychotherapists and sociologists. The fact that I call 'beautiful' the curves and lights of rock and sea in a North Atlantic bay can be explained by my particular 'psyche', with its particular ancestors. I remember taking the American explorer and scientist,

Stefansson, to that bay and saying: "A hard country, but beautiful". His response was to say how misleading it was to use such subjective language about terrain, and he proceeded to give me a lecture on modern geology and the modern discovery of 'objectivity'. In all scientific explanations we are required to eliminate the assumption of the other as itself beautiful. The platonic language which asserts that the world is beautiful and love is the appropriate response to it is believed to be based on a fundamental assumption of trust, because Plato was too early in the history of the race to have a proper scientific understanding of subjects and objects. That trust was shown to be a naive starting point by those who formulated doubt as the methodological prerequisite of an exact science.

Indeed the language of 'subjects' and 'objects' is one of the ways through which the beauty of the world has been obscured for us. This language was of theoretical use in the coming to be of technological science; one of its prices, however, was to obscure beauty. To state the literal meaning of 'objects' yet once again: it speaks of anything which is held away from us for our questioning. Any beautiful thing can be made into an object by us and for us and we can analyse it so that it will give us its reasons as an object. But if we confine our attention to any thing as if it were simply an object, it cannot be loved as beautiful. This is well illustrated in the division between useful and non-useful criticism by professors of literature and music who explicate the texts of works of art. For example, many such explications of Shakespeare or Mozart add to our understanding of the works concerned. But one central way of dividing the useful from the non-useful among such criticisms is the recognition by the critic that his work is a means to an end, which is the further understanding of the beauty of what is being studied.

When such writing appears stultifying, it is that the critic has stood over the thing studied and therefore the thing has remained an object. Its objectivity has not been a passing means but an end. (It may be said in parenthesis that such failed works often seem to appear because the professors concerned want to share the prestige of objectivity with their colleagues from the mastering sciences.) Only as anything stands before us in some relation other than the objective can we learn of its beauty and from its beauty. To say this may seem no more than a linguistic trick upon the use of the word 'objective'. But this is not so. The language of 'subject' and 'object' can easily suffocate our recognition of the beauty of the world. In stating that the beauty of otherness is the central assumption in the aphorism "Faith is the experience that the intelligence is enlightened by love", it is necessary to bring into consciousness the sheer power of the contemporary language of 'subjects' and 'objects', so that the statement is not killed by that language.

Indeed the central difficulty of using the language of beauty and love, in the affirmation that one knows more about something in loving it, is that in that language beauty was known as an image of goodness itself. Yet through the modern paradigm of knowledge the conception of good has been emptied into uncertainty. The first stage of this emptying was when good came to be used simply in discourse about human ethical questions. In the last century the emptying has gone farther. 'Good' has largely been replaced in our ethical discourse by the word 'value'. The modern emptying of 'good' can indeed be seen in the emptiness of its replacement. Even its chief philosophic originator, Nietzsche, has not been able to tell us what a value is. This vagueness has resulted in the word generally being used now in the plural— our 'values'.

At a time when the word 'good' has been so emptied of content by the modern paradigm of knowledge, it is necessary to proceed hesitantly in trying to say what it meant in relation to our love of the beautiful. It must first be stated that what was given traditionally in the word 'good' was not confined to Christians. The majority in the classical Mediterranean tradition would have so used it — Epicureanism being then a minority. A similar conception is in the Vedanta. Christianity's particular call was not to this language, but to the fact that Christ declares the price of goodness in the face of evil.

In the old language 'good' means what any being is fitted for. It is a good of animals to breathe; we are not if we do not. The good of a being is what it is distinctively fitted for. Human beings are fitted to live well together in communities and to try to think openly about the nature of the whole. We are fitted for these activities because we are distinguished from the other animals in being capable of rational language. In living well together or being open to the whole in thought we are fulfilling the purpose which is given us in being human, not some other type of animal. Good is what is present in the fulfilment of our given purposes. To avoid the modern view of temporality as futurity I use a different example. A child is good, not only as a preparation, but in so far as it is at all. One loves children for what they are now. In this sense the western word 'good' appears close to what the Vedanta means by the word 'ananda' (bliss) — not as a feeling, but as being itself.

At the heart of the Platonic language is the affirmation — so incredible to nearly everyone at one time or another — that the ultimate cause of being is beneficence. This affirmation was made by people who, as much as anybody, were aware of suffering, war, torture, disease, starvation, madness and the cruel accidents of existing. But it was thought that these evils could only be recognised for what they were if they were seen as deprivations of good. (It must be remembered that in this account of good and evil the verb "to be" is used differently from the way it is employed in most educated modern parlance.)

Clearly this language of the given goodness of what is must be a language founded upon trust. The archetypal expositor of this language, Socrates, knew that doubt was a necessary means to philosophy. But *The Republic* makes clear that such doubt is within the overreaching assumption of trust. We start with trust in our knowledge of those things we are presented with immediately, and doubt is the means of moving to an understanding of what makes possible that trust in an educated human being. The identity of doubt and systematic thought which lies in the origin of the modern experiment was not present in Socrates' enterprise. The modern assertion that what we are is best expressed as "beings towards death" would certainly have been in Socrates' mind in what he said at the time of his execution. But it was not for him the final word about what we are. At the moment when his death was immediate he made clear that we are beings towards good. It was indeed for this reason that in the scene of his death, Socrates asserts that the absence of knowledge of good is not ignorance but madness.

The central cause of the modern emptying of the word 'good' is that the new technological scientists defined the scopes and method of their activity in terms of their criticism of the old Aristotelian science, which had described things through the conception of purpose. The modern understanding of things in terms of necessity and chance, through algebraic method, has led not only to our conquest of nature, but to an understanding of things outside the idea of purpose. The successes of this method are a source of wonder (use the synonym 'admiration' if you will) to any sane person.

The new science (however one may sometimes flinch at what it says) had some appeal to certain Christians, in the very fact that it had defined itself against the teleological science of medieval Aristotelianism. When this science was used unwisely by official Christianity, in the name of ecclesiastical power, to assert that purpose in nature pointed to an overriding purpose given for the universe as a whole, it is understandable why many turned away from a science so triumphally used. The more representable the purpose of the whole was said to be, the more this natural theology became a trivializing, a blasphemy against the cross. Some of the most depressing episodes in Christian history have been the spilling of much silly ink to show that the universe as a whole vouchsafed a representable purpose of design analogous to the way that the purpose of the automaker is given in the design of the automobile.

Nevertheless, it is obvious that faith cannot turn away from the idea of good. Faith affirms that all that is, proceeds from beneficence. If faith is said to be the experience that the intelligence is enlightened by love, and love is said to be the apprehension of otherness as beautiful, then the question must arise whether this definition is not the kind of blasphemy of which I have been writing. Is it not saying that the beauty of the world gives us a representable purpose for the whole? Is it not just the kind of distortion which turns us from the facts of the world so that we seem able to affirm what is contradicted by the evident experience of living? Through it are we not led to assert that evil is good and good is evil, and so lose what is essential to any love of truth — namely the continual recognition that the world is as it is?

In writing about love of beauty, it is therefore necessary to say something of how the language of good and purpose is used about the beauty of the world without trivializing suffering. It is best to start from works of art, for here there is obvious purposiveness in that they are made by human beings, in some sense comparable to the automobile, in some sense not. They are both purposive in that means are arranged in the light of a purposed end. We can speak both of a well-made car and a well-made concerto. But it is certainly harder to represent to ourselves the purpose of the work of art. Certain works of art can be partially understood in terms of their well-defined external purposes. Bach's Passions were written to help believers focus their attention and their prayers around the originating events of Christianity. But when we turn to Bach's concerto for two violins it is less clear that we can represent its purpose.

Nowadays much of our time is filled by works of art. Their purpose is to entertain. Entertainment is the agreeable occupation of our attention—in the sense of what we happen to like. What was spoken in the Greek *techne* became the Latin *ars*. Plows and plays were both made by human beings and the making was named by the same word. In our world the activities called technical and artistic have separated between the practically useful and the entertaining. In both cases means are carefully adjusted to ends to produce a good car or computer, play or concerto. The skilful gathering together of means for the car is for the purpose of getting us around; in the play for the agreeable occupation of our attention. This account is everywhere in democratic capitalistic societies.

It is against this account of art that it is necessary to write. It stands between us and any proper apprehension of works of art, and ruins our partaking in their beauty. The purpose of a car can be represented rightly as a means of getting us around; the purpose of a work of art is not properly represented as merely entertainment. Indeed the greater the work of art the less can its purpose be represented at all. The staggered silence with which we can watch *King Lear* is evidence that something of great import is before us. Afterwards we can study it so that we can better understand the parts in relation to the whole. Whether watched or read, it clearly has a purpose. When we are enraptured we can say that it seems purposiveness itself. But can we ever represent that purpose to ourselves? Who has been able to tell us what is the purpose of *King Lear*? In a certain sense the purposiveness is nothing but the gathering together of the means employed by its author; in another sense its purpose is present but we cannot represent it. The beautiful at its heights gives us purposiveness but its good transcends us (oh dangerous word). It is not chiefly entertainment that we have consumed when we are consumed by great beauty.

This is well illustrated in the non-verbal and non-representational language of music—for example in the last piano concertos of Mozart (let us say numbers 14 to 27). It is clear that these are purposive in the sense that the techniques of Italian and German music are here supremely used. It is also clear that we partake in their purpose the more we are able to follow the intricacies of modulation and counterpoint, and understand the unity between the three movements of each work. We can be aware of the moods of majesty and gaiety and desolation which are expressed in the music. We can also know that Mozart needed to entertain the Austrian upper classes to make money. Entertainment is occupying our attention agreeably. But with what? To some cultures and to some people their attention is more agreeably occupied by *Rhapsody in Blue* than by K.482. This fact raises inevitably the question: are there some works that are more worth paying attention to than others? What is given in those that are most worthy of attention? What is it that enraptures us about them, so that even in the desolation of *King Lear* or K.491 we are enraptured? Can we describe that enrapturing as the immediate engrossment in the beauty of the work, which points to good which is quite unrepresentable?

Here indeed one must pay attention not only to looking or reading or listening, but to the very making of such works. To do so would be a staggering impudence, had not the activity been described by Mozart himself.

> The question is how my art proceeds in writing and working out great and important matters. I can say no more than this, for I know no more and can come upon nothing further. When I am well and have good surroundings, travelling in a carriage, or after a good meal or a walk or at night when I cannot sleep, then ideas come to me best and in torrents. Where they come from and how they come I just do not know. I keep in my head those that please me and hum them aloud as others have told me. When I have that all carefully in my head, the rest comes quickly, one thing after another; I see where such fragments could be used to make a composition of them all, by employing the rules of counterpoint and the sound of different instruments etc. My soul is then on fire as long as I am not disturbed; the idea expands, I develop it, all becoming clearer and clearer. The piece becomes almost complete in my head, even if it is a long one, so that afterwards I see it in my spirit all in one look, as one sees a beautiful picture or beautiful human being. I am saying that in imagination I do not understand the parts one after another, in the order that they ought to follow in the music; I

understand them altogether at one moment.
Delicious moments. When the ideas are discovered and put into a work, all occurs in me as in a
beautiful dream which is quite lucid. But the
most beautiful is to understand it all at one
moment. What has happened I do not easily forget
and this is the best gift which our God has given
me. When it afterwards comes to writing, I take
out of the bag of my mind what had previously
gathered into it. Then it gets pretty quickly put
down on paper, being strictly, as was said, already
perfect, and generally in much the same way as it
was in my head before.[4]

The combination expressed in these words between the
free work of the artist and his receptivity allows us dimly to
perceive what that wonderful making must have been.
Obviously his mastery of technique has come from long
training and attention. We know that the last piano concertos were written after he had studied Bach, late in his short
life. His own hard work is united with his receiving of
melodies and his hearing of the whole piece all at one
moment. Fire has always been the word to describe love,
and it has been written that flame touches flame. The
making of a beautiful piece is an act of love, a love which
illuminates the lucidity in his making of it.

Two points may be made, not to add anything to these
words, but because the dominant language in modern
education may cut us off from listening to the words. First,
it has been a central theme in modern philosophy that
there is no such thing as 'intellectual intuition'. This has
gone with the teaching that the great mistake of the Platonic tradition has been the affirmation of such. 'Intuition'
comes from the Latin *tueor*, to look. When Mozart says that
after composing a piece of music he sees it 'all in one look'

and when he says he understands it all at one moment, he is surely describing an act which can properly be named 'intellectual intuition'. Secondly, it is worth remembering when Mozart speaks of understanding (in German the very similar word *verstehen*) he did so at a time when Kant was exalting reason above understanding, in the name of his account of human beings as 'autonomous'. This was to place on its head the teaching of Plato in which understanding is the height for human beings. Indeed the English 'to understand' and the German *verstehen* were in their origins filled with that very sense of receptivity which Kant lessens in the name of our freedom.

Critics who write within the historicist assumptions of our time might choose to deconstruct this letter in one way or another. They say that Mozart's music is a different matter from his justifying explanation of his understanding of it. At another level it might be said in languages of modern physiology and psychology that the language of gift and the fire of love can now be better understood for what they are than in Mozart's 'naive' words. Indeed with our new knowledge it may be said that we will be able to add to the Mozartian corpus by means of the computer. Mozart's assertion that he understood the whole of a piece in one look and heard it all at one moment can only be wiped away if we speak entirely within the languages of the new sciences. What has been lost as against what has been found in the self-definition of the modern paradigm here appears to me evident.

What can be meant by the beauty of the world becomes more ambiguous when we pay attention to those things which have not been made by human beings. At a common sense level, Vico's insistence that we understand what we have made in a way we cannot understand what we have not made seems correct. More importantly, it is difficult to partake in the beauty of the world because of the misery, the hardness, the sadness of so much of our lives, which is caused not only by the ugliness in ourselves, but by the very conditions of the non-human world. As has often been said, the very drive to technological science arose with the desire to overcome these vicissitudes. The key difficulty in receiving the beauty of the world these days is that such teaching is rooted in the act of looking at the world as it is, while the dominant science is rooted in the desire to change it.

I am not saying that the beauty of the world is vouch-safed above all when untouched by human making. It would be senseless to think of cultivated land as unbeautiful. Race horses are beautiful. Nevertheless, it was possible for Canadians to admire the chthonically beautiful places, where nature existed untouched by human making, and moreover to see these places as beautiful even in the awareness of how rigorous pioneering society had been — my ancestors, for example, were forced to eat the flesh of their dead companions to survive. In the western world today, fewer and fewer people can ever find nature untouched by technological science. On His return, it may not be understandable for Christ to repeat what He said about the lilies of the field, because if there are any lilies they will have been improved by human skill. For most people, animal existence appears as cats and dogs, meat to be eaten or wild animals protected in zoos or wilderness areas. The heavens, the oceans and the mountains are as yet only partially conquered and the heavens may be at points untouchable. Indeed the beauty of the world in its primal sense is rarely present for us, and that assertion need not depend on the ambiguous doctrine of 'the Fall'. It is indeed necessary to call modern science 'technological' because in the modern paradigm nature is conceived at one and the same time as algebraically understood necessity and as resource. Anything apprehended as resource cannot be apprehended as beautiful. At some stages of our capitalist development, certain rhetoricians used to say: "Canada's greatest resource is its people". That well-meaning sentence expresses what has been lost as well as found in modernity.

Of course the beauty of the world manifests itself most intensely for us in the beauty of other people. The manifold forms of love, for example sexual and parental, friendship and admiration, take in each case many forms themselves. Who could in a lifetime write down the ways in which sexual love penetrates every moment of our consciousness and is never absent in any loving of the beautiful —present even when that love is universal?

Indeed the manifold ways in which sexual instinct and love are held together and detached from each other make up much of our existing. On the one hand, sexual desire can be the recognition of others as beautiful; on the other hand, it can be the occasion of such calculated self-engrossment that other people are made instruments for producing sensations. Sexual desire can be the occasion when we see the truth of what others are, in the flame of its attention; or it can lock us in the madness of ourselves so that nothing is real but our imaginings. So intense are the pleasures of sexuality, so pressing its needs, so detached can the bodies of ourselves and others be from any humanity, that sexual desire can drive love out from its presence. It can become the rock of 'reality' on which the search for the beauty of the world founders.

In an age in which the paradigm of knowledge has no place for our partaking in eternity, it is understandable that orgasmic fulfilment has been made out to be the height of our existing—indeed that which gives our existing some kind of immanent justification. The materialists have taken it as their heaven. But this modern union of individuality and materialism has meant a transposition of older beliefs about the relation of sex and love. In the older beliefs sexual desire was one means through which love between human beings could abound; in our era love seems sometimes to be thought of as means for the abounding of sexual enjoyment.

Because sexuality is such a great power and because it is a means to love, societies in the past hedged it around with diverse and often strange systems of restraint. Such restraints were considered sacred, because their final justification (whatever other justifications were present) was the love of the beautiful, and that was considered sacred. Modern social scientists have changed the original meaning of "taboo" into the socially and psychologically "forbidden", in the attempt to teach us that restraints are not sacred. This is of course useful to a capitalist society because everything must be made instrumental to the forwarding of 'production', and the sacred restraints cannot be made instrumental. Social scientists follow their creator, because social science was created by capitalist society.

It is the reversal in the hierarchy of love and sex which has led in the modern world to the attempt to remove the relation between sexuality and the birth of children. The love of the beauty of the world in sexual life was believed to have some relation to the love of the beauty of the world found in progeny. (In using the word 'some' before 'relation', I imply that I am not speaking against contraception). But if orgasmic fulfilment is the height of all existing, it has no need of such extension. Obviously, love has to be protected by societies, because the human condition is such that the tenderness of the flesh leaves everybody at the terrible mercy of others. Yet at this time in 'advanced' societies, justice has been massively withdrawn from unborn children.

In the pre-progressive societies, however differently (and often perversely) love was brought within different orders, those loves were not considered entirely blind, because they were the way that human beings were moved out of self-engrossment to find joy in the world. Indeed the words 'to love' and 'to know' were joined. For example, because of the intensity and intimacy of orgasmic love, it was said when people freely participated in it, they 'knew' each other. Love was not considered in its essence blind. It was for this reason that the family—in such varied forms as polyandry, polygamy, monogamy, etc.—was given enormous power (sometimes indeed too much) because it was believed that in the main the family was a guardian of the interests of its members.

Indeed one of the growing beliefs of our era is the idea that love in its essence is blind. For people of my generation the great teacher in matters sexual and familial was Freud. He seemed a writer who gave sexual life its central place after the repression of the early industrial era. But for all his concentration on love, he (like his master Nietzsche) gave love poison to drink, because he so placed ambiguity at the centre of love as to say that in its heart love was blind. His influence may not be intellectually lasting. But he has been influential, particularly in North America, in placing sexual and familial life under the hands of the objectifiers. The 'helping' professions—psychiatrists, social workers etc.—are an important means of bringing people under that objective control. This is largely done by the claim that they understand families better than the families understand themselves.

Luckily many people are not much interested in such assumptions and just go on loving or being indifferent or hating. But deep changes in ways of looking at things slowly permeate, particularly in societies whose democratic origins were bound up with the idea that philosophy could be open to nearly everyone. Thus when a populariser of philosophy such as Sartre writes that "hell is other people", he makes starkly open the modern division between love and intelligence.

The results of the division of love and intelligence are evident when one speaks of knowledge of justice. In the older tradition, justice was defined as rendering to anything what was its due. Political justice was the attempt to render what was due among human beings. For ourselves, justice was rendering what was due to every aspect of our own being, body and soul, as we were then considered to be. In the non-human world it was rendering the proper due to cattle and bears, wheat and stones, to God or the gods. Justice was then not only arrangements to be realised in any given society, but also a state of the individual which was called a virtue. Of course the question arose to thought, why is anything due to anything? Once any due had been granted, the question came to be what was properly due to any being. Socrates shows in his debate with Callicles in *Gorgias* that life demands the idea of due. He then proceeds in *The Republic* to show how we come to know what is due to anything.

What Christianity added to the classical account of justice was not any change in its defintion but an extension of what was due to others and an account of how to fulfil that due. Christ added to the two great commandments the words that the second is "like unto" the first. At the height of the Gospels we are shown the moment when a tortured being says of his torturers that their due is to be forgiven. Despite all the horrors perpetrated by Christians, both in the west and more particularly outside the west, despite all the failures of Christians to understand the consequences of justice for the law, nevertheless the rendering to each being its due, in the light of the perfection of that rendering, could not be publicly denied among Christians. Indeed Christianity calls human beings not only to the reasonable decencies of the particular purposes and goods of this or that situation, but to be perfect as God in heaven is perfect. There is no short cut to this perfection by a mysticism without price. As Simone Weil says, "Matter is our infallible judge." Perfection is not isolated from the immediate requirements of the world. We can only fulfil those requirements here below insofar as we partake to some degree in that perfection. Indeed goods in the here and now are only good in that they participate in goodness itself. Our freedom is just our potential indifference to such a high end.

Indeed among all the western criticisms of Christianity the most substantial was that Christianity led to over-extension of soul. It was said that too much is demanded of human beings and this has made steady political orders impossible where the Gospel was influential. The call to perfection made difficult the handling of the necessities of the world, and laid too grave a burden upon individuals. This criticism and the replies to it were both made by people who accepted that justice was rendering each being its due.

The call to perfection caused the persecution of the saints, not only in communities alien to Christianity (*e.g.*, in the early Roman Empire or in modern secular empires) but in the heart of what was known as Christendom. The call to perfected justice seemed to question the elementary justice possible in the world. The harsh imprisonment suffered by St. John of the Cross was administered at the hands of church-men because of his desire to fulfil the original Franciscan perfection. The intelligence's enlightenment by love is a terrible teaching (in the literal sense of the word). Contemplate what happens to those who have been deeply illuminated by love! After the resurrection

Christ told Peter that he must expect to be carried "whither he wouldst not". In the traditional teaching about justice it was recognised that human nature is so constituted that any desire which has not passed through the flesh by way of actions and settled dispositions appropriate to it is not finally real in the soul. The saints are those in whom the desire for justice has so passed through the flesh that it has become transparent to justice.

The very call to perfection in Christianity has been above all that which has made so difficult the establishment of proper systems of government. The compromises between the world and perfection were particularly necessary in this area. "Render unto Caesar the things that are Caesar's; and unto God the things that are God's" is a brilliant epigram, but hard to particularise. In any given society where Christianity has been influential only few hear the call to perfection and who those few may be is not easy to specify. Most of us make something of trying in a half-hearted way to render others their due. Some lose all sense of others having any due. For most of us it is easier to envisage the unrepresentable end for those near and dear to us. It is harder to envisage it even among those in the same neighbourhood, let alone farther away. Love of the good due to others can easily become little more than love of our own. Saddest is when love of our own becomes no more important than love of our own bodies and our own immediate needs.

It was recognized that the wicked were not alone the individual criminals, but those who wished to rule for their own self-assertion. Such people were more destructive of justice even than those who ruled simply in terms of the property interests of one class. They were worse than those who climbed the slippery pole of politics to get some place of influence. Because such tyrants were the most dangerous for any society, the chief political purpose anywhere was to see that those who ruled had at least some sense of justice which mitigated self-assertion.

For these reasons there were in the pre-progressive societies those complicated systems of education wherein the truth of justice was made central to education. Indeed, the pressing reason for this is given with startling clarity by Socrates in *Phaedrus*. For most of us justice must initially appear as unattractive. Justice is not easy to be loved because it is not, at first sight, beautiful. Socrates also says that the more we come to love it the more we come to find it beautiful. Indeed it has been recounted by those advanced in the journey that justice which once appeared ugly or tiresomely distracting comes to appear as overwhelmingly beautiful.

As traditional societies were economically limited and therefore the possibilities of education were directed to the few, it was to those most likely to rule that this education was given. Among the young, the cultivation of habit was considered central. Justice was, in its origins, good habit. The early practice of fulfilling some small segment of justice was necessary to the overcoming of self-assertion among the young. For those likely to rule this was not sufficient. It was necessary to understand justice within the whole scheme of the cosmos. When one compares the education of Queen Elizabeth the First, or of Gladstone, with that given to nearly all modern rulers, one may come to understand why they were such masters of what Plato called the highest art. Is there anything greater in modern politics than Gladstone's attempt in his last years to turn England back from the absurdities of expansionist imperialism, which were leading directly to the disaster of 1914?

In our history this education in justice depended greatly on the careful division of function between church and state. The state was concerned 'ideally' with the immediate instituting of justice in the world; the church was 'ideally' concerned with holding high perfection in its cosmic significance, and with the education which proceeded therefrom. Obviously at nearly every moment each of these institutions abused their proper functions and trespassed on each others prerogatives. Indeed, whatever the difficulties in understanding the origins of technological society in the Christian west, one of the moments where its origin is evident lies in the activity of the pope whose popular name was Hildebrand. In this controversy with the empire, Hildebrand not only insisted on the spiritual rights of the church, but also on the control of the world, by the papacy's power over the naming of the emperor. By this vast extension of the church's power over the world, he turned the church from its traditional role of holding forth the mystery of perfection, to the role of control in worldly affairs. The apparatus of education in the church was turned to the world, including the activity of thinkers. We should not be surprised that Swift's *Battle of the Books* places Thomas Aquinas among the moderns, not the ancients.

The accounts of justice which have become dominant during the age of progress have not been based on its definition as rendering each being its due. This has happened largely because it has not been widely thought in our age that we can have knowledge of what is due to each being. An analogy has often been used to describe the central difference between pre-progressive and progressive theories of justice. In all theories of political justice it must be assumed that some limitation is placed on individual liberty. In the traditional theories this limitation was vertical, received by human beings in what they knew about the whole, which quite transcended any individuality. What was given in our knowledge of the whole was a knowledge of good which we did not measure and define, but by which we were measured and defined. The modern theories depended on a horizontal limitation, which arose from the fact that one human being's right to do what he wanted had to come to terms with the right of others to do what they wanted. The basis of society was the calculation of the social contract wherein sensible human beings calculated that all had to surrender some part of their unlimited desire for freedom in order to enjoy the benefits of settled society. This contractarian view of the state was as much part of communism through the dependence of Marx upon Rousseau, as it was part of American democratic capitalism through the founders' dependence on Locke's rights to 'life, liberty, and property'. In *Perpetual Peace* Kant put the matter lucidly. He wrote that it would be possible to have a just society composed of a nation of clever devils. If they were smart enough to negotiate the social contract, they could have a just society.

As it is my intention to state that something has been lost for us with the waning of the old account of justice, it is well to think about what has been gained in and through the modern accounts. Some examples: whatever the differences in theory or application between democratic capitalism and communism, clear statements about equality were present in both theories. And before one ever speaks against equality, it is well to remember what it was like for those at the bottom of the ladder when the principle of equality was modified by the principle of hierarchy. It is bad enough for those at the bottom of the ladder under our systems, but at our best this cannot be justified by theory. Or again: Locke was the chief philosophical progenitor of the American pursuit of 'life, liberty, and property' and he said what he said about government because he thought the end of life was comfortable self-preservation. It is well to remember how much comfortable self-preservation is a key end in life. The modern union of contractarianism and technological science has, despite all the terrors of modernity, added to many people's 'comfortable self-preservation'. Or again: the question can be formulated by saying that the pre-progressive thinkers said virtue was the core of a just political order, while the moderns have given freedom that position. It is well to remember how much all of us want to do what we want to do, and do not want to be interfered with by others, particularly when that interference is in the name of some virtue which seems completely alien to us.

Nevertheless, it seems necessary to state what has been lost theoretically in the modern definitions of justice. What has been lost is the belief that justice is something in which we participate as we come to understand the nature of things through love and knowledge. Modern theories of justice present it as something human beings make and impose for human convenience. This is done in a physical environment which is understood in terms of necessity and chance. Obviously the traditional belief, as much as the modern, included cognizance that human beings were responsible for doing things about justice. Human beings built cities, empires, etc. and some regimes were better than others. To use the favourite expression of the Enlightenment, human beings have in modernity taken their fate into their own hands. Their theories of justice teach them that our institutions are what we make in terms of our own convenience.

The central cause of this great change has been modern natural science. Brilliant scientists have laid before us an account of how things are, and in that account nothing can be said about justice. It is indeed not surprising therefore that in the coming to be of technological science the dependence of our objective science upon calculus has been matched by the dependence for knowledge of justice upon calculation. When the world is understood as necessity and chance, then justice has to be made by the 'authentic' freedom of human beings, so that conflicts between our pleasure seekings can be worked out. It is not surprising that those studies in our multiversities which depended on our intelligence being enlightened by love, and which were publicly sustained because they taught people to participate in justice, should now have faded into antiquarian research. After all it is not very difficult to know these days what justice is, what beauty is. The first is the result of interested calculation; the second is the means of entertainment.

II

In discussing the dominance of our modern paradigm of knowledge in the multiversities, I do not intend to make yet another list of goods and ills which have come forth from that paradigm. Who cannot be grateful for the electric light; who cannot be aware that physics has made potential the destruction of all life on this planet? To make such a list would not only require many volumes, but also assume some common agreement about goods and ills. But it is the very possibility of such a common agreement which is at stake. My purpose is rather to illustrate the pressure that people of faith must feel if they attempt to live intellectually serious lives in the multiversities. There are many of us who have found that our intelligences have been enlightened, however poorly, by love. Some of us have contact with the educational system and find that what we are taught there as knowledge is in disaccord with what we know in faith. (That old chestnut again!) There are many good ways for Christians to live with the modern paradigm of knowledge. I am concerned here as one of those who find themselves trying to live seriously in the multiversity.

It is not unwise to start such pondering from the science of Darwin. Not only have his discoveries had a determining effect on modern biology, not only have these discoveries made difficulties for people of faith for more than a century, but also he was an English-speaking person and we are the people who have won the wars so far in this century. It is therefore apposite to put the question of faith and the multiversity in an English-speaking setting. This appositeness can be seen in some English scientists suggesting recently that 1859—the date of the publication of *Origin of Species*—should be called Year 1, in replacement of the A.D. dating of the older paradigm. This would be more universally accepted by the world as a whole.

First two quotations: one about Darwin, the other by him. A friend who talked with him in the countryside wrote: "Nothing escaped him. No object in nature, whether Flower, or Bird, or Insect of any kind, could avoid his loving recognition." Darwin wrote to another friend in 1887: "Personally, of course, I care much about Natural Selection; but that seems to me utterly unimportant, compared to the question of Creation or Modification."

In writing of these two statements it is not my chief purpose to discuss at length the strange way that the great scientist brings together creation and modification as if they were alternative answers to the same question. Yet in parenthesis something must be said on this matter to clear the way for the central point I wish to make. Obviously modification, if described as taking place as natural selection, adds force to Laplace's dictum: "je n'ai pas besoin de cette hypothèse". But modification *per se* (that is as held apart from natural selection) does not so strike against the teaching of creation. The teaching about creation in theology has been one answer to the question: why is there anything rather than nothing? Modification is an answer to the question of how species came to be in this world. In saying this, two points must be emphasised. (1) The question 'why is there anything rather than nothing?' is an abyss in which our minds are swallowed up. That it is an abyss easily leads to the modern assertion that it is not a real question, and therefore not worth thinking about. It is worth repeating that the recent power of the English-speaking peoples has encouraged human beings to ignore that question. (2) The doctrine of creation is not the only answer to this abysmal question; the eternity of the visible universe is another.

Be that all as it may, my purpose is to ask what is being spoken about life in Darwin's great synthetic discoveries, and the relation of what is there spoken to the possibility of knowledge from the beauty of the world. Obviously no one who is thoughtful can contemplate living beings without some clarity concerning the modification of species by natural selection.[5] When we look at the tumult of the cormorants among their young on a rocky island, or the sea silver with mackerel, we know that if we were trained we could come to be clearer about the modifications of these species and the ways in which the mechanisms of natural selection have worked among them. We can know that the mackerel are a resource like electricity or metals, and we know that we do not have to get rid of the cormorants as it is necessary to get rid of rats in war. Is there anything else we can know? Is there anything else that we need to know for these animals to continue to be? A less immediate example:

we are now often shown in our homes beautiful pictures of species in many parts of the world. While watching these pictures we are generally told by some biologists how the presence of these beings is to be understood in terms of the modifications of natural selection. Often when the species is known to be 'endangered' we are given a sermon by the biologist on saving this species. But nothing is said of anything that can be known as to why we should be glad that there are polar bears or parrots or why they are worth working to preserve. Some of these may be resources for this or that, but it is hard to see why some species are resources for anything. They are of course a tourist resource and we will be able to see certain species of birds in aviaries. As they have come to be by the chancy necessities or perhaps necessitous chances of natural selection, is there anything that we can be told of why it is good that they are and continue to be? The Portuguese used to leave plague-infected clothes covered with trinkets for the natives of Brazil, and (lest this should be thought xenophobic) there are no surviving natives on the island of Newfoundland.

To write of the quotation of Darwin's friend: what is the relation between his 'loving recognition' of the beasts and flowers and what he cognised about them? It may well be said that what he knew about them means that no educated person should ever recognise them again in the same way people once did. But the question remains: is Darwin's love of the beings expressed in what he discovered about them? This is not to deny that he must have rightly loved his own remarkable act of synthesis, but that is a different thing from his love of the beings themselves. What was the relation of his love for them to what he discovered about them (and indeed about us)? To love something with intelligence is to want it to be. What is it about the animals as the product of modification through natural selection which would make us want them to be?

It is not extreme to point out that the era in which Darwin's explanations have had such power in the life sciences has also been the era in which human beings have been responsible for the destruction of more species than at any other period. Obviously Darwin did not invent the repeating rifle; nor was he on the Board of Dow Chemical. Nevertheless at a simple level it must be said that there is some connection between what we think other species to be (let alone our own) and how we treat them. Facts and values are not so disjoined as we have been led to believe. At a deeper level it may also be said that the same technological destiny brought forth Darwin's science and the human conquest of the environment.

It is more important, however, to ask: what is the relation between Darwin's loving recognition, as reported by his friend, and what Darwin discovered about the animals? Obviously that 'loving recognition' was connected to the disciplined attention necessary to his discoveries; but what was discovered about them therein does not itself call forth love for them. To know that human and non-human species are modified through natural selection gives us a greater clarity about ourselves and others. We may indeed love the clarity and comprehensiveness of the formulation. But that which is known in the formulation provides us no reason to find beautiful that about which the formulation is made. It gives no reason why we should love ourselves or other animals. Can we love ourselves and others just because we have come to be through natural selection? The beauty of the world is not in the dominant modern formulation concerning life.

The example of Darwin has been used because it is a leading illustration of the deep disjunction which has fallen on western existence — the disjunction between beauty and truth. What we experience as beautiful in what we make, or in what we do not make, is cut apart from what we know about things in science. (I must avoid the language which would speak of 'art or nature', because the greatest English writer was able to say 'the art itself is nature'). This disjunction of beauty and truth is the very heart of what has made technological civilisation.

In one of his last writings, Nietzsche stated this disjunction with great certainty.

> If my readers are sufficiently initiated into the idea that "the good man" represents, in the total drama of life, a form of exhaustion, they will respect the consistency of Christianity in conceiving the good man as ugly. Christianity was right in this.

> For a philosopher to say, "the good and the beautiful are one" is infamy; if he goes on to add, "Also the true" one ought to thrash him. Truth is ugly.

> We possess art lest we perish of the truth.[6]

The force of Nietzsche's rhetoric may seem here to exaggerate when he says that truth is ugly. Indeed there are many truths which must seem to nearly everybody ugly. Darwin's discoveries about natural selection do not make the animals ugly, but neither do they tell us why the animals are beautiful. The modern disjunction between the true and the beautiful is made particularly evident in saying that scientific propositions are 'value neutral' or 'value free'.

Obviously people go on loving otherness because they find it beautiful. The issue here is not whether this can cease to be while there are human beings. Rather it concerns what happens when there is a disjunction between their experience of some beings as beautiful and what they are taught about the truth of such beings in the modern paradigm of knowledge. What is the result when they cannot hold in unity the love they experience with what they are being taught in technological science? The results face us in nearly every important circumstance of our lives. One public consequence is given in Nietzsche's sentence "We possess art lest we perish of the truth." The avidity for the consumption of art in mass societies is an obvious fact. Yet the distinction I have made previously between art and entertainment can be interpreted unfairly concerning what happens in mass societies. The desire for entertainment, understood in the squalid terms of utilitarianism, is not all that holds people to the production and consumption of art. There is also the hope to find in it meaning in a world where beauty and truth have been publicly disjoined. The question still remains, however, whether this hope can be sustained when artists know, if they are at all educated, that the beauty they are bringing forth is disjoined from the truth of what is. Keats' apparent platitude has often been ridiculed, but it allowed him to bring forth beautiful poems in great physical difficulty. Can we possess art when we perish of the truth?

This disjunction lies at the heart of that paradigm of knowledge in which knowing and making are co-penetrated. Who can say what the world-wide dominance of that paradigm portends for the future? But something can be said of what it means for us Christians in the here and now. It could not be my competence to say what it means for fellow Christians in all the manifold occupations and occasions of society (that would be impertinence). But I have spent my life in multiversities, and therefore can speak about what this disjunction means for believers in that context. Yet even within this small compass, I do not intend to write of practical problems.[7]

Rather, what I am concerned with is the dominance of this paradigm over the intellectual life of any university which is left in the multiversity. Many students come to our multiversities with some belief from outside the modern paradigm. Obviously I am not speaking here solely of Christian traditions and what they hand over of the eternal. Indeed it is easy to think that in the long haul it may be the Vedanta which is most resistant to destruction by technology. But in Canadian universities the chief lingering is Christianity. In most cases that lingering remains as the residual remembrance of morality. To quote again the English vulgarian: Matthew Arnold said that "religion is morality tinged with emotion". In their decadence certain western Christians even suggest that that silly definition is true.

The young who come to the multiversity from some tired tradition may not be much concerned with any discussion of 'faith and the multiversity'. They can accept the dominant paradigm with open arms because it is their ticket to professionalism and that is the name of the game. Rather I am concerned with the group at the multiversity with some sense of the eternal good which is God, and perhaps even some sense of the declaration of that eternity in Christ. For such men and women, the facing of the modern paradigm in its incarnation will be fairly direct, because they cannot take it as sufficient if they hold what they have been given of eternity.

For people in this situation it is fortunate to have the capacity for reflection. This is not to say that reflection is the chief means of coming into the presence of eternity. We have been clearly told that it is not. Nor is reflection a capacity open to many. Nor is it a capacity confined to the intellectually bright with high IQs. For example, it seems clear that most scientists do not need to reflect. Indeed the very practice of the modern paradigm may turn them away from reflection. To do their work successfully generally inhibits them from reflecting on the paradigm within which their work is done. Nevertheless, in as intellectually broken a society as ours, it is good fortune to have the capacity for reflection. But in some ways not. There are loyal Christians (called by their critics 'fundamentalists') who generally say that 'technology' is not a paradigm of knowledge but a set of instruments— inventions which come from scientific discoveries. As a whole, they do not much reflect on the ontological implications of the modern paradigm. They therefore live with certainty in the modern. Such people often make crude mistakes in theory; but who does not? Nothing fills me with greater aesthetic annoyance than the scorn which has been heaped on such people by clever journalists and 'intellectuals' (whatever that word may mean).

With or without the capacity for reflection, those who come to the multiversity with some memory, some intuition, some dense loyalty for the eternal good are faced with the modern paradigm which excludes the possibility of any such. They are faced with the implications of that exclusion the more their studies lead them to enter the truth of the paradigm. This has led to terrible diremptions.

Dostoevski wrote to Madame von Wisine: "I believe that there is nothing finer, deeper, more lovable, more reasonable, braver, and more perfect than Christ; and not only is there nothing, but there cannot be anything. More than that; if anyone told me that Christ is outside truth, and if it had been really established that truth is outside Christ, I should prefer to stay with Christ than the truth." But that came from a man who had been brought up surrounded by orthodoxy, who had spent his terrible exiled imprisonment with only the Gospels to read and who wrote the most substantial criticism of the West that I am aware of. The possibility that there is a disjunction between the entirely beautiful and the truth, and Dostoevski's certainty that he would stay with Christ, is declared by a great man who had lived on the limits of suffering. But for the most of us who do not and could not live on such heights, this disjunction between beauty and truth can be killing. For the young who really enter the multiversity it may kill them in the losing of those memories, those intuitions, those loyalties to the eternal good.

The woman who wrote the definition of faith from which I have proceeded, once also wrote: "One can never wrestle enough with God if one does so out of pure regard for the truth. Christ likes us to prefer truth to him because, before being Christ, he is truth. If one turns aside from him to go towards the truth, one will not go far before falling into his arms." That is a great hope given us by a woman who had pure regard and who had gone far. But did she, in the sheer force of her intellect, know how much the rest of us can be diverted by the modern paradigm from that fearful wrestling—and indeed from the pure regard? How is it possible to think that the modern paradigm is sufficient to the needs of human beings? And yet how is it possible, in the midst of that paradigm and its stranger and wilder consequences, to reach into the truth that the world proceeds from goodness itself?

Appendix

Questions about the history of thought arise concerning this writing. (1) Why 'use' the language of a great philosopher—in this case Plato—to describe Christianity, when the Gospels are little concerned with philosophy? (I put the word 'use' in quotation marks because philosophy always uses the user rather than he or she using it.) (2) Is it not absurd and antiquarian to write now of Christianity in the language of an ancient philosopher (albeit the greatest)? Would it not be wiser to 'use' the language of a modern philosopher?

(1) The permutations and combinations of the relations that have been between Christianity and philosophy could make up a whole history of the western world. It is not my business to write ten or more volumes about the history of those permutations and combinations. To speak of them elementarily: it is clear that Christianity is as much "the

practice of dying" as Socrates said that philosophy was. When we turn to either we come quickly upon the two great deaths which stand at the origins of western life and thought. Yet these two deaths are very different. The calm, the wit, the practice of thought which are present at Socrates' death may be compared with the torture, the agony, the prayers, which are present in Christ's death. Just before drinking the hemlock Socrates makes a wonderful joke; in Gethsemane Christ's "sweat was, as it were, great drops of blood falling to the ground". Indeed the difference is also stated in the fact that where Socrates' wife is absent for most of *Phaedo*, the two Marys stand beneath the cross.

Yet it is apposite that in his attempt to invert Platonism and to mock Christianity Nietzsche should have said: "Christianity is Platonism for the people." The greatest nineteenth-century thinker was right to understand that the establishment of the highest modernity required not only the liberation of the west from Christianity, but also from Platonism, because of the deep connection between the two. At the beginning of his exoteric work, *Beyond Good and Evil*, this aphorism lays down the closeness between Christianity and Platonism. It can free the mind from all the nonsense of the assumption, in so much Biblical scholarship, that the achievement of such doctrines as the Incarnation and the Trinity were just mistakes of the Church fathers because they had wanted to Hellenise the Gospels. However much Christ's life and death and resurrection were the events of divinity, human beings had to think their relation to other events. Because Platonism asserts the primacy of Goodness itself, it was considered the best language for this task.

The close connection between Socrates and Christ lies in the fact that Socrates is the primal philosophic teacher of the dependence of what we know on what we love. In the

central books of *The Republic*, Plato uses the image of the
sun, the line and the cave to write of the journey of the
mind into knowledge. In those images sight is used as a
metaphor for love. Our various journeys out of the shadows
and imaginings of opinion into the truth depend on the
movements of our minds through love into the lovable.
Indeed there are many ways of thinking about Socrates'
'turn around' from interest in such phenomena as the clouds
to his later interest in human matters. But one of these is
his recognition of the interdependence between knowing
and loving.

This relation between Christ and Socrates is denied by
those who would distinguish absolutely between two Greek
words for love, *eros* and *agape*. Paul's hymn to love uses the
word *agape* which is best translated as charity; Plato's symposium is concerned with *eros* which is best translated as
desire. Even as sweet-blooded a popular theologian as C.S.
Lewis distinguishes between what he calls need-love and
gift-love, which in their essence become for him desiring
and charity. Obviously it is the case that there is a great
range between my liking for scrambled eggs, and Francis
loving the lepers. (Let alone all those eccentric and crazy
desires that seem to make up the substance of most of our
lives.) There are clearly very different kinds and examples
of love. But this does not seem reason to draw too sharp
distinctions between them, and in so doing deny that all
love is one.

Needs always imply something needed, and therefore
the love of what is needed — good or bad. Human beings
are in their essence needing beings, and when otherness
has become completely absent for us, we are hardly human
beings at all. It must be emphasised that for Plato the
opposite of knowledge is not ignorance, but madness, and
the nearest he can come to an example of complete madness

is the tyrant, because in that case otherness has disappeared as much as can be imagined. On the other side, does not
the giving of oneself away which we call charity imply
some need in that giving? Is it not clear among the saints
that they are not simply bestowing on others something by
writ, but because they have seen what these others are?
When charity is without *eros* it can become administrative
dictate—however necessary the administration. A consequence of charity without need on the part of the charitable
was expressed to me by a friend about the retarded and
disabled: "How would you feel if everybody you had dealings with were paid for those dealings?"

Indeed those who rigorously disunify love by distinguishing need-love from gift-love and so place *eros* on the
side of philosophy and *agape* on the side of Christianity,
should remember the fable in *Symposium*. Eros was begot-
ten at a celebration for the birth of Aphrodite. The parents
were two beings called Fullness and Need. Eros not only
goes around as a beggar but is in itself the activity of
begetting upon the beautiful, both in bodies and souls. At a
western height, Francis was able to beget upon the lepers as
beautiful.

Of course the metaphor of sight as the need of otherness
is combined with the metaphor of light which allows us to
see. The philosophy of the dialogues is impregnated with
the idea of receptivity or as was said in the old theological
language, grace. What is given us and draws from us our
loving is goodness itself; the perfection of all purposes
which has been called God. We are hungry for the bread of
eternity. In a way which is almost impossible to affirm, let
alone describe, we can trust that we are offered such bread.

In much modern thought the core of being human is
often affirmed as our freedom to make ourselves and the
world. Whatever differences there may be among Chris-

tians about what it is to be human, finally there must be the denial of this account of freedom. Whatever we are called to do or to make in the world, the freedom to do and to make cannot be for us the final account of what we are. For Plato freedom is not our essence. It is simply the liberty of indifference; the ability to turn away from the light we have sighted. There is no word in Greek which can be translated into the modern word 'ideal'. The modern use of 'ideal' means the opposite of 'real'. 'Ideals' are those thoughts in our heads by which we make ourselves and the world what we think they ought to be. In this essential matter of what human beings are, Platonism and Christianity are at one, as against the thinkers of 'authentic' freedom. To exist is a gift.

Of course, for both Christianity and Platonism, goodness itself is an ambiguous mystery. In Christianity, God's essence is unknowable. In *The Republic* it is said that goodness itself is beyond being. Both Christianity and Platonism have therefore often been ridiculed as final irrationality. If the purpose of thought is to have knowledge of the whole, how can we end in an affirmation which is a negation of knowing? It is, above all, these agnostic affirmations which bring Platonism and Christianity so close together. Without this agnosticism humans tend to move to the great lie that evil is good and good evil. In Christian language this great lie is to say that providence is scrutable.

(2) Why not turn to the language of a modern philosopher to present Christ in relation to all that is? The chief argument for so doing would be that the great event between ancient and modern philosophy was Christianity, and therefore most modern philosophy is impregnated with Christian language (even if only in the form of secularized memory). Would it not therefore be wise to use such modern language to explicate the relation of Christ to all that is?

My answer to this argument would be in one word—Heidegger. His writings make up the profoundest and most complete modern philosophy—certainly the deepest criticism of ancient thought which has ever been made in the name of modernity. Yet it is a philosophy which excludes something essential to Christianity. Heidegger writes that Nietzsche's dictum "God is dead" means that the God of morality is dead. Now indeed Christianity is not morality; nor is it "morality tinged with emotion." Nevertheless we have been told, "Blessed are those who hunger and thirst after righteousness." 'Morality' is indeed a boring word; but finally it is the same as 'righteousness'. If God who calls for righteousness is dead, then Christianity's God is dead. Do we think that we know better than Heidegger what he means, and thus use him to write about Christianity? But if not Heidegger, whom? He speaks more comprehensively and more deeply than any modern philosopher.

It is not wise to criticise Christianity in public these days when so many journalists and intellectuals prove their status by such criticism. Nevertheless it seems true that western Christianity simplified the divine love by identifying it too closely with immanent power in the world. Both Protestants and Catholics became triumphalist by failing to recognise the distance between the order of good and the order of necessity. So they became exclusivist and imperialist, arrogant and dynamic. They now face the results of that failure.

Modern scientists, by placing before us their seamless web of necessity and chance, which excludes the lovable, may help to reteach us the truth about the distance which separates the orders of good and necessity. One of Nietzsche's superb accounts of modern history was that Christianity had produced its own gravediggers. Christianity had prepared the soil of rationalism from which modern science came, and its discoveries showed that the Christian God was dead. That formula gets close to the truth of western history, but is nevertheless not true. The web of necessity which the modern paradigm of knowledge lays before us does not tell us that God is dead, but reminds us of what western Christianity seemed to forget in its moment of pride: how powerful is the necessity which love must cross. Christianity did not produce its own gravedigger, but the means to its own purification.

Nietzsche and the Ancients: Philosophy and Scholarship

I

It is with an ambiguous mixture of approval and hesitation that one reads an article by the Regius Professor of Greek at Oxford on "Nietzsche and the Study of the Ancient World".Professor Lloyd-Jones begins by speaking of "the unfortunate prejudice which for most of this century has prevented most American and English people from recognizing the immense importance of this writer."[1] The purpose of this article is to explain my ambiguous reaction, not only because the relation of Nietzsche to the study of the ancient world is intrinsically interesting, but also because it can be used as a paradigm through which to look at the current relation between scholarship and philosophy. The pedagogical question as to why we should encourage students to

read Nietzsche turns into the more important question as
to how we can teach students to read Plato from out of
non-historicist assumptions.

It is easy to state the cause of immediate pleasure in
Lloyd-Jones' article. He makes amends for all the misinterpretation and disregard of Nietzsche which has taken
place in the English scholarly world. I simply repeat the
bare outline of the story of that misinterpretation in
Germany and England. When Nietzsche published *The
Birth of Tragedy* in his twenties, the German scholar Wilamowitz launched a series of attacks on Nietzsche's scholarship, from which he drew the conclusion that his account of
Socrates was not to be taken seriously. Wilamowitz's position had only a short run in Germany, because the relation
between philosophy and scholarship was too deeply rooted
in that society. After 1900 it was difficult for educated
Germans to avoid Nietzsche's conclusion that those who
faced the consequences of scientific positivism were likely,
if they were moderns, to become historicist existentialists.
Nietzsche's portrait of Platonism was clearly a keystone in
the thinking of that historicism. He had stated that scientific and philosophical rationalism had come forth from that
arch-seducer, Socrates, as a means of turning away from
what was given in the art of tragedy. Now, after more than
two thousand years of dominance, that rationalism had
produced in modern science and scholarship the means of
overcoming itself. Human beings had at last the means of
living beyond its seductions. Because of the power of Nietzsche's statement of historicism in German intellectual life,
the accusation that his account of the ancient world was
unscholarly did not have much influence in Germany in
this century. It had some influence, however, in that Heidegger took the opportunity to answer it at the beginning of
his thousand page commentary on Nietzsche. Heidegger is

not a writer much given to the use of wit, but he uses the high style of comedy in ridiculing those who claim that there is no need to read Nietzsche because he is not a respectable scholar.[2]

The situation in the English-speaking world was different. That world was entering politically the stage of open competition between itself and Germany—the competition which was to lead to two massive world wars. Everything German, having once been praised, was becoming suspect. Moreover, the English-speaking societies had so long dominated the political world, first in the power of Great Britain and later in that of the U.S.A., that they were immensely confident of their own traditions, which were those essentially of contractual liberalism. Societies which are so confident of their power in the world have little need of philosophy. "The owl of Minerva only begins to spread its wings in the dusk". Therefore there was every reason for English-speakers to disregard what Nietzsche had written. The British classical scholars ridiculed or disregarded Nietzsche. The analytical philosophers made out that he was some kind of romantic rhetorician who disregarded the evident truth of modern science and wrote in a style so turgid as to be beyond the pale. This assessment was given added justification when Nietzsche was taken up by the most immoderate and indeed perverted side of the German political spectrum—the national socialists. Nietzsche's doctrine of the *Übermensch* could be taken, by those who did not need to read him, as a precursor of the most vulgar racism. Nietzsche was accused of the anti-Semitism which had been present in the intellectual gutters of Europe, and he was accused of it even in the light of his arguments that it was a terrible contemporary disease, and even when almost his last written words were a cry for the destruction of that gutter anti-Semitism. (How interesting it is that Frege is taken as a central founder of mathematical logic, and his wild anti-Semitic diatribes forgotten by the analytical philosophers. Nietzsche, who spoke early in the 1870s and 1880s of European anti-Semitism as a secular disease of terrible portent, has been condemned in England as a racist.) This mixture of misinterpretations made Nietzsche a ridiculed, unread and even proscribed writer in the English-speaking world.

Lloyd-Jones says that he is a classical scholar and not a philosopher (whatever that may be in the current English-speaking context). Nevertheless he has read Nietzsche, not only in his early stage as a classical philologist, but also the main body of writings when he had given up that occupation. For those of us who do not know the details of the history of philology in Europe, Lloyd-Jones is clear about Nietzsche's place in the various academic schools and their quarrels. He is particularly interesting about Nietzsche's early philological writings from the time of his professorship at Basle. He clears out the negative political prejudices of the English world. But he is chiefly interested in Nietzsche as the man who first set in motion the movement of scholarship which was concerned with 'the irrational' in Greek civilisation,

> ...the great movement that culminates, or seems to us to culminate, in *The Greeks and the Irrational* of E. R. Dodds...Nietzsche saw the ancient gods as standing for the fearful realities of a universe in which mankind had no special privileges. For him what gave the tragic hero the chance to display his heroism was the certainty of annihilation; and tragedy gave its audiences comfort not by purging their emotions but by bringing them face to face with the most awful truths of human existence and by showing how those truths are what makes heroism true and life worth living.

In comparison with such an insight, resting on a
deeper vision of the real nature of ancient religion
and the great gulf that separates it from religions
of other kinds, the faults of Nietzsche's book, glar-
ing as they are, sink into insignificance. (p. 9)

One is grateful for this summary of what Nietzsche said
about ancient polytheism in the *Birth of Tragedy*. Yet the
gratitude is accompanied by disquiet for the following
reasons. How far does Lloyd-Jones want to go with Nietzsche? What will be the effect of bringing Nietzsche onto
the stage of English-speaking classical scholarship, especially if it be inevitable that he enter centre stage? It is
obviously proper for Lloyd-Jones to limit himself to the
influence of Nietzsche on classical scholarship. But the
question remains: as classical scholarship is but part of
knowledge of the whole, can Nietzsche's influence be
limited, even within that scholarship itself? As Nietzsche
wrote in his extremity: "After you had discovered me, it
was no trick to find me; the difficulty now is to lose me."[3]
This raises the more general question of the relation of any
historical scholarship to philosophy. In any sane educational system (and I am not implying that the North American system is that), scholarship must see itself not as an
end, but a means in the journey of minds towards the truth
concerning the whole. Moreover, any scholarly activity is
carried on by human beings who come to know what they
know about the past in terms of some assumptions about
the whole, that is in terms of some partaking in philosophy,
however inexplicit. Nietzsche is above all the thinker who
first laid before the western world the doctrine of historicism radically defined. This teaching has now become the
dominant methodological principle underlying most contemporary scholarship. I mean by historicism the doctrine

that all thought (particularly the highest) depends, even in its very essence, upon a particular set of existing experienced circumstances—which in the modern world we call 'history'. Nietzsche gave us his account of the ancient gods within that historicism, and understands that account as part of the 'truth' of that historicism. The question then is whether one can limit his influence upon classical scholarship to the recognition of his interpretation of 'irrationalism' in Greek religion.

The tensions in the relation between modern scholarship and philosophy are illustrated in E. R. Dodds' *The Greeks and the Irrational,* which Lloyd-Jones praises so highly. Dodds' book is a fine product of a long life of scholarly reading among a wide variety of ancient authors. It lays before the reader many aspects of Greek life which had not been emphasised by the scholars who looked at the world through the eyes of a dying 'idealism'. To a political philosopher such as myself, whose central reading is not with such authors, and yet who wishes to have knowledge of the ancient world, the book brings much that is not otherwise available. Nevertheless, the facts are presented from out of an assumed British liberalism as that creed was expressed by decent Oxford gentlemen. Dodds goes so far as to identify very closely the 'rationalism' of fifth century Athens with nineteenth century English 'rationalism'. How far that goes may be seen when he identifies Socrates in *Protagoras* with Jeremy Bentham (p. 211). Indeed in such an identification, the gap between scholarly and philosophical reading is startlingly present. Also, by the twentieth century, Oxford gentlemen were talking more openly about sex in their scholarship, and Dodds continually refers to his debt to Freud. But Dodds' Freud is essentially a therapist of sexual difficulties whose view of human life is well contained within British liberalism. The book ends with a peroration that western 'rationalism' (by this he means the English variety) may be able to save itself from 'the failure of nerve' which caused the end of Athenian rationalism, because we have the advantage of Freudian therapy which will allow us to come to terms with our irrationalism and contain it within our rational tradition. This final peroration is appropriate because it was presented first as lectures in California during the 1950s. At that time, the wisdom of American academia insisted on the close alliance of liberalism and psychoanalysis. Dodds' Oxford Freud is not far from the Y.M.C.A. Freud prevalent in his day in the U.S.[4]

The difficulty of such Freudianism united with a good-willed theory of democracy is that one doctrine of man takes over the private realm, while another is asked to rule in the public. Such a compromise may be practically acceptable in a society for a short span, but in the longer term such elementary inconsistency becomes apparent even to busy public men. Why should constitutional regimes be considered superior to their alternatives if human beings are basically 'ids'? It is well to remember for the purposes of my present argument that it was not Freud but Nietzsche who first and most consistently expounded the doctrine that human beings are 'ids'. Although Dodds' book provides the reader with interesting facts about the classical world, the mish-mash of ultimate presuppositions makes the book a confused read for a political philosopher.

Because Lloyd-Jones praises Dodds as the culmination of classical scholarship about the 'irrational' in an article praising Nietzsche's influence in the same field, one cannot leave alone the jumble of assumptions within which Dodds carries out that scholarship. The mixed assumptions raise the question of the relation between classical scholarship and philosophy. They also raise the question of what happens to classical scholarship if it takes philosophy as

Nietzsche takes it. I hope it will not be considered imper-
tinent trespass for somebody in 'another field' to touch this
subject.

It seems true to this outsider that classical studies before
the Enlightenment were considered chiefly valuable as the
necessary preparation for the study of philosophy. This
study was allowed by rulers, not because it was thought
intrinsically good, but as a necessary preparation for
political judgement and theology. The study of Homer,
the dramatists and the poets was secondary to this end. In
short, classical studies were sustained in the great tradition
of rationalism—above all because they led to the study of
Plato and Aristotle. Whatever else Nietzsche's writings
may be, they must be taken as the most sustained, the
deepest and most comprehensive criticism of that great
tradition. The depth of that criticism is sustained throughout all his writings in his pondering on Socrates as the
great seducer. From this follows his comprehensive attack
on Plato. The purpose of classical scholarship must surely
become very different if that comprehensive attack is taken
as successful. In this sense the thought of Nietzsche cannot
be taken as something that contributes to classical scholarship within a given account of what that scholarship is. It
must be taken as something which, if true, will change the
purposes of that activity fundamentally.

What will be the place of classical scholarship in our
universities as historicism becomes more articulate in the
English-speaking world? In some ways historicism seems a
closer friend of Greek studies than the long tradition of
positivism which preceded it, and in which positive classical scholarship stood on one side and philosophy on the
other, and the gap between them increasingly widened.
Historicism has been both a cause and effect of that
engrossment with the human past which so characterises

our best modern universities, and which is supported in our societies because of the desire to understand our inheritance in the midst of a fast changing world. This engrossment guarantees the continuance of chairs of classics. In this sense, historicism seems a friend of classical studies. Also historicism, in its grandeur in the thought of Nietzsche and Heidegger, recognises that we as westerners come forth from Socratic rationalism above all, and therefore educated men should study Greek philosophy to understand what they have to overcome.

Yet at a deeper level one may ask whether such historicism is really the friend of classical studies. What is the effect on classical studies when crude historicisms in anthropology and archaeology teach that it is equally illuminating to the young to study the Incas and Philistines as to study Greek civilisation? Among the various historicist substitutes for philosophy, anthropology now adds its name to that of sociology, economics and psychology. Classical studies will continue in the universities not only because they have been there, but because among the vast variety of past societies Greece and Rome are accidentally our own. But our own will be less important amidst the smorgasbord of the past. In such an atmosphere, classical studies will be further detached from the conception that they bring something unique to be known, and will increasingly be concerned with filling out the details of the past (setting Thucydides right, as the expression goes).

To repeat, among the articulate historicists there will be a continuing interest in Plato and Aristotle because we can understand ourselves only in terms of the 'problem' of Socrates. But this study of the ancients will be a kind of modern therapy—the understanding of them so that we can free our minds of that rationalism of which they were the origin. For the highly educated, that historical therapy is necessary to allow them to become authentic moderns.

Socrates turned away from tragedy (and what was given in its truth about sexuality) in saying that what was final was not the abyss, but good. The greatest achievement of modern scientists and philosophers was the destruction of Greek rationalism with its 'substances', its 'truth' and its 'good'. The greatest height for man was laid bare in Greek tragedy, in that it made plain that the basic fact of existence was our encounter with an abyss—our encounter with the finality of chaos. Classical rationalism is seen as a species of neurotic fear, a turning away from the elementary fact of the abyss by means of a shallow identification of happiness, virtue and reason. Our study of it must therefore be a kind of historical therapy (similar to the way Nietzsche proposes to free us of Christianity). That therapy is a means for the educated to bring themselves to an even greater height than that proclaimed in tragedy. It will be a greater height because it will now take into itself both the primacy of the abyss and the overcoming of chance made possible through scientific technology. This will enable the great and the noble to be 'masters of the earth'. The combination of the primacy of the abyss with technology will produce the *Übermensch*—those who will deserve to be the masters of the earth. Humanity has been a bridge in evolution between the beasts and those who are higher than human beings. Nietzsche may have been the great political critic of Rousseau, but he accepts his account of human origins. Reason does not open us to the eternal; its greatness has been to transcend itself in its modern manifestations, so that we are both enabled and deserve to be masters of the earth. Nietzsche is not an 'anti-technological naturalist', but one who believes that modern technology has allowed a new height for men.

For this reason one looks with fear as well as pleasure at praise of Nietzsche from the Regius Professor of Greek.

There is some truth in Lloyd-Jones' statement that Nietzsche was a valuable inspiration to classical studies because he turned attention to the irrational. But is it possible to take Nietzsche in this context and not take him seriously as the most sustained critic of Plato? What will happen to classical studies if they are even further removed from their traditional role as a means to the truth to be received in the study of classical philosophy? If this study is a therapy to allow us to realise that modern philosophy has freed us from the power of Socratic rationalism, will not this further weaken the power of classical studies in western society? The Greeks will be our Incas which we study for their mythology. Already in the English-speaking world analytical philosophy has done much to weaken the study of ancient philosophy. The discovery of the irrational among the Greeks may through its historicism seem to enliven an interest in classical matters. But will this interest be of sustained seriousness when it is undertaken within existentialist historicism? It is this which makes one think that the praise of Nietzsche from Lloyd-Jones (and others like him) is a Janus as far as the future of classical studies is concerned.

II

There is no escape from reading Nietzsche if one would understand modernity. Some part of his whole meets us whenever we listen to what our contemporaries are saying when they speak as moderns. The words come forth from those who have never heard of him, and from those who could not concentrate sufficiently to read philosophy seriously. A hundred years ago Nietzsche first spoke what is now explicit in western modernity. When we speak of morality as concerned with 'values', of politics in the language of sheer 'decision', of artists as 'creative', of 'quality of life' as praise and excuse for the manifold forms of human engineering, we are using the language first systematically thought by Nietzsche. At the political level his thought appears appropriately among the atheists of the right; but equally (if less appropriately) it is on the lips of the atheists of the left. When we speak of our universities beyond the sphere of exact scientific technologies, what could better express the general ethos than Nietzsche's remark: "Perhaps I have experience of nothing else but that art is worth more than truth." And of course radical historicism is everywhere in our intellectual life. It even begins to penetrate the self-articulation of the mathematicised sciences.

In such circumstances there is need to read Nietzsche and perhaps to teach him. One must read him as the great clarion of the modern, conscious of itself. If the question of reading Nietzsche is inescapable, the question of whether and how and to whom he should be taught is a more complex matter. It is particularly difficult for somebody such as myself, who in political philosophy is above all a lover of Plato within Christianity. The following story is relevant. A man with philosophic eros was recently asked the rather silly question: "At what period of time would you best like to have lived?" He answered that he was lucky to have lived in the present period, because the most comprehensive and deepest account of the whole has been given us by Plato, and the most comprehensive criticism of that account has been given us by Nietzsche. In the light of that criticism, one can the better understand the depth of Platonic teaching. That is, one should teach Nietzsche as the great critic of Plato. The difficulty of reading Plato today is that one is likely to read him through the eyes of some school of modern philosophy, and this can blind one. For example, many moderns have in the last century and a half followed Kant's remark in the first Critique that he was combining an Epicurean science with a Platonic account of morality. With such spectacles how much of Plato must be excluded? The great advantage of Nietzsche is that such strange combinations are not present. His criticism of Plato is root and branch. In the light of it the modern student may break through to what the Platonic teaching is in itself.

Nevertheless, the teacher who is within the philosophic and religious tradition, and who also takes upon himself the grave responsibility of teaching Nietzsche, must do so within an explicit understanding with those he teaches that he rejects Nietzsche's doctrine. If I were not afraid of being taken as an innocent dogmatist, I would have written that one should teach Nietzsche within the understanding that he is a teacher of evil. The justification of such a harsh position is difficult, particularly in universities such as ours in which liberalism has become little more than the pursuit of 'value-free' scholarship. This harsh position is clearly not 'value-free'. Moreover, such a position is ambiguous in the light of the fact that I do not find myself able to answer comprehensively the genius who was the greatest critic of Plato. But there is no need to excuse myself. Who has been able to give a refutation of radical historicism that is able to convince our wisest scientific and scholarly friends?

Without such capability, what is it to say that one should teach within the rejection of Nietzsche? Is not this the very denial of that openness to the whole which is the fundamental mark of the philosophic enterprise? Is it not to fall back into that dogmatic closedness which is one form of enmity to philosophy? I will attempt to answer that by discussing Nietzsche's teaching concerning justice. As a political philosopher within Christianity, my willingness to teach Nietzsche within an understanding of rejection, while at the same time I am not capable of the complete refutation of his historicism, turns around my inability to accept as true his account of justice. At least we need have no doubt as to what Nietzsche's conception of justice is, and the consequences of accepting it.

A caveat is necessary at this point in the argument. I am not making the mistake that is prevalent in much condemnation of Nietzsche—namely that there is no place for justice in his doctrine. His teaching about justice is at the very core of what he is saying. To understand it is as fundamental as to understand the teaching concerning "the eternal recurrence of the identical". It is said unequivocally in a fragment written in 1885, towards the end of his life as writer.

> It happened late that I came upon what up to that time had been totally missing, namely justice. What is justice and is it possible? If it should not be possible, how would life be supportable? This is what I increasingly asked myself. Above all it filled me with anguish to find, when I delved into myself, only violent passions, only private perspectives, only lack of reflection about this matter. What I found in myself lacked the very primary conditions for justice.[7]

This quotation does not give content to Nietzsche's conception of justice. Its nature appears in two quotations from the unpublished fragments of 1884. "Justice as function of a power with all encircling vision, which sees beyond the little perspectives of good and evil, and so has a wider advantage, having the aim of maintaining something which is more than this or that person." Or again: "Justice as the building, rejecting, annihilating way of thought which proceeds from the appraisement of value: highest representative of life itself."[7]

What is the account of justice therein given? What is it to see "beyond the little perspectives of good and evil"; to maintain "something which is more than this or that person"? What is "the building, rejecting, annihilating way of thought"? What is being said here about the nature of justice would require above all an exposition of why the superman, when he is able to think the eternal recurrence of the identical, will be the only noble ruler for a technological age, and what he must be ready to do to "the last men" who will have to be ruled. That exposition cannot be given in the space of an article. Suffice it to speak popularly: what is given in these quotations is an account of justice as the human creating of quality of life. And is it not clear by now what are the actions which follow from such an account? It was not accidental that Nietzsche should write of "the merciless extinction" of large masses in the name of justice, or that he should have thought "eugenical experimentation" necessary to the highest modern justice. And in thinking of these consequences, one should not concentrate alone on their occurrence during the worst German regime, which was luckily beaten in battle. One should relate them to what is happening in the present western regimes. We all know that mass foeticide is taking place in our societies. We all should know the details of the eugenical experimentation which is taking place in all the leading universities of the western world. After all, many of us are colleagues in those universities. We should be clear that the language used to justify such activities is the language of the human creating of quality of life, beyond the little perspectives of good and evil.

One must pass beyond an appeal to immediate consequences in order to state what is being accepted with Nietzsche's historicist account of justice. What does a proper conception of justice demand from us in our dealings with others? Clearly there are differences here between the greatest ancient and modern philosophers. The tradition of political thought originating in Rousseau and finding different fulfilments in Kant and Hegel demands a more substantive equality than is asked in Plato or Aristotle. What Hegel said about the influence of Christianity towards that change is indubitably true. But the difference between the ancients and the moderns as to what is due to all human beings should not lead us to doubt that in the rationalist traditions, whether ancient or modern, something at least is due to all others, whether we define them as rational souls or rational subjects. Whatever may be given in Plato's attack on democracy in his *Republic*, it is certainly not that for some human beings nothing is due. Indeed to understand Plato's account of justice, we must remember the relation in his thought between justice and the mathematical conception of equality.

In Nietzsche's conception of justice there are other human beings to whom nothing is due—other than extermination. The human creating of quality of life beyond the little perspectives of good and evil by a building, rejecting, annihilating way of thought is the statement that politics is the technology of making the human race greater than it has yet been. In that artistic accomplishment, those of our fellows who stand in the way of that quality can be exterminated or simply enslaved. There is nothing intrinsic in all others that puts any given limit on what we may do to them in the name of that great enterprise. Human beings are so unequal in quality that to some of them no due is owed. What gives meaning in the fact of historicism is that willed potentiality is higher than any actuality. Putting aside the petty perspectives of good and evil means that there is nothing belonging to all human beings which need limit the building of the future. Oblivion of eternity is here not a liberal-aesthetic stance, which still allows men to support regimes the principles of which came from those who had affirmed eternity; oblivion of eternity here real- ises itself politically. One should not flirt with Nietzsche for the purposes of this or that area of science or scholar- ship, but teach him in the full recognition that his thought presages the conception of justice which more and more unveils itself in the technological west.

Research in the Humanities

The words 'arts faculties' and 'humanities' are unclear and ill-thought terms by which to describe the grouping together of certain studies. Nevertheless, the word 'humanities' is the present convention. The chief conflict of roles among the best young professors in the humanities is the same as that in other faculties—the conflict between the demands of teaching and administration on the one hand, and the demands to produce research on the other. There is, however, one great difference between the situation in the humanities and in the other faculties. Research in natural science, medicine, engineering, law, and even the social sciences has significance for the best professors and students, and is related closely to the life of the society they inhabit. Research in the humanities can less and less be seen as having any significance by the best professors and students. This is because it is oriented today towards a 'museum culture,' not to knowledge necessary to human existence. A recent president of the University of Toronto announced a book about that university entitled *Half Way Up Parnassus*. You will remember that Parnassus is the home of the muses. An inaccurate title. The Robarts library is not the home of the muses, but their mausoleum, where they are preserved as Lenin in the Kremlin. And this is even truer of the universities in the United States which Canadians now imitate. I use the metaphor 'museum culture' because museums are places where we observe past life as object. This present situation is clear in the strange fact that at one and the same time never has so much money been put into the organized study of the past and never has the past had less meaning in our lives.

Why is it that humanities research produces only this irrelevant museum culture? The overriding reason is of course that any high culture other than technology is now simply epigonal in Europe, and high culture in the U.S. is an epigone of these epigones, and we in Canada are in turn an epigone of the U.S. But I want to take one simple point from that destiny—the strange marriage which has taken place between scholarship and research. In any sensible university, scholarship has always been considered a useful means. It has recently been raised to a sacred word to be spoken of in a fruity voice reminiscent of the sanctuary. When human beings are oblivious of eternity, they always make false things sacred. But beyond this false sacralization of scholarship, a deeper process has been going on—a change in the very nature of scholarship itself because of its marriage with research.

What then is given us in the word 'research'? All societies are dominated by a particular account of knowledge and this account lies in the relation between a particular aspiration of thought and the effective conditions for its realization. Our account of knowledge is that which finds its archetype in modern physics with all the beauty given in the discoveries of that science. Our account is that we reach knowledge when we represent things to ourselves as objects, summonsing them before us so that they give us their reasons. That requires well-defined procedures. Those procedures are what we call 'research'. What we now mean by research is not then something useful for some ways of knowing and not for others. For us it belongs to the very essence of what we think knowledge is, because it is the effective condition for the realization of any knowledge. Research and team research have produced and will continue to produce extensive results in the progressive sciences.

What happens when the procedures for ordering objects before us to give us their reasons become dominant in 'humanities' scholarship? The very procedure of research means that the past is represented as an object. But any thing in so far as it is an object only has the meaning of an object for us. That is why it is quite accurate to use the metaphor of the mausoleum about our humanities research. Moreover when we represent something to ourselves as object we stand above it as subject — the transcending summonsers. We therefore guarantee that the meaning of what is discovered in such research is under us, and therefore in a very real way dead for us in the sense that its meaning cannot teach us anything greater than ourselves. This is why scholarship as research has changed the very meaning of the word. As Heidegger has shown so clearly, the place that experiment plays in the progressive sciences is taken in humanities' 'research' by the critique of historical sources. Previous scholarship was a waiting upon the past so that we might find in it truths which might help us to think and live in the present. Research scholarship in humanities cannot thus wait upon the past, because it represents the past to itself from a position of its own command. From that position of command you can learn about the past; you cannot learn from the past. This stance of command necessary to research therefore kills the past as teacher. The strange event is this: the more the humanities have gained wealth and prestige by taking on the language and methods of the progressive sciences, the less significance they have in the society they inhabit.

In the minds of many generous natural scientists 'the humanities' are believed to be part of the traditional university, and as such they generously support them. But the assumption they start from is not a fact. The humanities research which is being realized in Canada is not to be identified with the traditional university. It comes forth from intercourse between two very untraditional partners: the post-Nietzschean nineteenth-century German university which mounted American capitalism. In emphasizing that our model is German I am simply pointing out that in intellectual fields particularly, the destiny of technological cultures was first made manifest in Germany, and was an enormous break with the European past. The mating of the German model of the university with American capitalism produced in the fifties its Chicagos and Berkeleys and Yales. Now in the 1970s we are producing our imitations of these in English-speaking Canada. Poor old Canada is enthusiastically taking on the American wave in its decadence. I have no right to speak of French-Canadian universities, but I have the right to point out that if their administrators think they are going to be saved from this by their relation with France they should remember that the intellectual culture of France has been increasingly dominated by the same necessary technological forces.

What then happens to bright young humanities professors in 'the museum culture' they are asked to reproduce?

The best of their students think they are going to get something living from the humanities, and when they find they are not, opt for the real culture which is all around them. Outside the official university, there is the real culture of the movies, popular music, and polymorphous sexuality. But there is no relation between the culture of the humanities and the popular culture. The first sterilizes the great art and thought of the past; the second is democratic but at least not barren. Which would you choose? Within the university there is the real culture of exciting research which truly does progress in the natural sciences, medicine, law, the social sciences, etc.... The young humanities professor must be productive in the industry he is part of; but he must teach students who are not often held by the museum research which the professor must turn out for his promotion. If the teacher is at all bright, he probably wants more from life than to be a junior executive in 'the past' industry. For this reason all across North America those of the clearest mind and noblest imagination are leaving the humanities in droves. They leave the field more and more free to the technicians who have narrow but intense ambitions to build careers in this industry.

It is all to easy to be comic about the way our scholarship industry lays European 'civ' before us in a form appropriate to intellectual tourists. What is more constructive is to try to think why its practitioners believe that their work is of such value. To make that attempt would be above all to think why we westerners have believed since Rousseau that there is a realm of being called 'history' and to try to understand what the science of that realm was supposed to teach us. It will have to be thought if the humanities are to escape their present busy and well-paid decadence.

This decadence (where high ends end in museums) is a civilizational destiny which can be little shaped by the activities of university administrators or of government officials. But in thinking about the university of the future, administrators must inevitably be faced by this problem: where are those questions going to be 're-searched,' the answers to which cannot be found in the modern sciences of nature or of history? I take for granted that such questions belong to human beings as long as there are human beings. If these questions are to be thought about within our universities, this will not be much done within the humanities faculty. If not there, where in the university? If not in the university, where in our society? Happily the eternal can take care of itself and therefore these questions, however difficult, are not easily avoided.

The Language of Euthanasia

with Sheila Grant

I

During the last decade there has arisen on this continent a
new threat to the traditional account of life and death.
Some forms of mercy killing have become acceptable to the
public conscience, and there is pressure for these to be
widely extended. The idea is not new, but the restraints
that held it in check have been severely weakened.

It cannot be stressed too strongly that the occasions on
which euthanasia is being considered as a possible option
are likely to be full of anguish and complexity for those
concerned. They may be suffering from all kinds of con-
tradictory pressures. The time when they need good judgement may be the time when they are least capable of it,
being swamped with grief and fear and guilt. Doctors are

in a position to exert extreme influence, as they alone have all the medical facts, are responsible for their interpretation, and are authority figures to begin with. But however agonizing the decisions in particular cases, the rest of us do nobody any service by refusing to make judgements about euthanasia with as clear an eye as possible. The distinction must be made: one must judge acts but never human beings.

What makes discussion of this subject so difficult is that there is a great public confusion about terminology. The word 'euthanasia' means literally 'a good death', something we all want. The current meaning of the word is "deliberate intervention to bring about the death of another human being", usually because the life of that person is judged valueless. Mercy killing was the old word for this practice, but it is not now always appropriate, as mercy is not always the motive for the killing. In this writing we will use the word 'euthanasia' as it is now employed.

It is first necessary to distinguish euthanasia from certain perfectly valid medical practices which are often confused with it. The use of large doses of pain killing drugs may have the side affect of somewhat hastening death, but are given to alleviate pain. This is not euthanasia, as its purpose is not to procure death. Another procedure is the refusal to initiate or continue life-supporting treatments, such as respirators, on those who are already in the process of dying. To prolong dying is not a doctor's duty, and has never been considered good medical practice. The current temptation for doctors to do this arises because they now have such good machines.

It must be forcefully stressed that the proper refusal to prolong inevitable death is quite different from deliberately causing the death of someone who is not already dying. Only the latter is euthanasia. Yet this confusion is widespread. The usual response to an expression of disapproval of euthanasia is: "So you want to keep all those poor old people on respirators indefinitely." In March of 1980 there was a C.B.C. talk show that went like this:

> *Interviewer:* "Now doctor, tell us what euthanasia is."
> *Doctor:* "It's killing—because you feel somebody's life isn't worth living."
> *Interviewer* (reproachfully): "Are you sure you don't mean letting someone die with dignity?"
> *Doctor:* "No, that is quite different."

The interviewer immediately turned to keeping the dying alive, and confusion reigned for the rest of the programme.

If the public rightly disapproves of the abuse of technology on the dying, yet wrongly identifies euthanasia with letting the dying die, then our attitude to euthanasia inevitably becomes more positive. The sacredness of human life becomes overlaid in the muddle as to what euthanasia is and is not. The old distinctions about euthanasia, direct and indirect, active and passive, also obscure more than they illuminate. We will concentrate on the three kinds of euthanasia most used nowadays: (a) voluntary, (b) involuntary killing of aged or comatose people, and (c) "benign neglect" of infants (which is also of course killing).

Voluntary euthanasia occurs when a patient asks a doctor or relative to end his life, generally with a lethal drug. It is often called "assisted suicide". It is not the same as refusing treatment, which is the right of any patient. Suicide is no longer illegal in Canada, but assisting suicide is. So it is not surprising that we have little definite information about the frequency of this kind of euthanasia. Most doctors would presumably try to put a patient out of his misery, not by killing him, but by relieving his pain and fear, which may be all he actually wants. There have been no requests for euthanasia at hospices and palliative care units. Voluntary euthanasia is being encouraged by societies such as "Exit" in England, and "Hemlock" in California. "The right to die" is called for. In a book published by "Exit" it is suggested that there are only two ways of dying with dignity—by voluntary euthanasia or by suicide. Those who are ready to approve of the "right to die" in our laws may not realize until too late that what they are in fact encouraging is the "right to kill".

Adult involuntary euthanasia takes place among those who for reasons of age, incurable disease, coma, or partial brain damage have a life expectation of very low quality. The future of such patients may involve mental deficiency, pain, hospitalization and expense. We do not know how often this kind of euthanasia is done, though we know that it is done. Although most of the medical profession are at present against it, there is strong public pressure for its legalisation. The slogan, as Heather Morris suggests, may well be "Every granny a wanted granny".

In these cases, methods of omission are likely to be used rather than a lethal injection. Ordinary life support may be removed, such as intravenous feeding from a patient who cannot eat enough by mouth. Or life supporting equipment, such as respirators or dialysis machines, may be withdrawn from patients who are not dying, and who need them. (To repeat, this is not to be confused with the removal of a machine from a dying patient whose condition cannot be improved by it.)

The law still calls it homicide to bring about the death of a patient; but in the US since 1976, the courts have begun to use "quality of life" judgements in decisions concerning death. Extensions of this basis of judgement may eventually cover large segments of the population —such as the mentally retarded, whose life expectation is, by definition, deemed of low quality, and therefore perhaps not worth preserving.

The third kind of euthanasia, now established and prac- tised widely on this continent, is the medical management of defective infants by killing a selection of them. The practitioners call it "benign neglect", which sounds better than infanticide. This is the most extreme development yet. It is carried out and written about quite openly. It meets very little opposition. The courts stand aloof, the public is largely indifferent, the medical profession divided. In 1971 the Johns Hopkins hospital made a movie about the 15-day starvation of a Down's syndrome baby, whose parents did not accept their retarded child. Since then respectable hospitals in the US and Canada have announced in the press that this is their practice. Articles in praise of this method of starvation have been written in medical jour- nals and popular magazines.

Another method of "benign neglect" used much in England, is slower but somewhat less painful than straight starvation. The baby is sedated and given glucose and water when he or she wakes and cries. As heavily sedated babies do not cry very often, they die in something under 3 weeks.

Proponents of euthanasia talk much about children who are mere vegetables. This term usually refers to anenceph- alic babies, born without an upper brain. They will die whatever we do or do not do. Their prognosis is quite clear at birth. As they only live a few days or a few weeks, and do not suffer, and as only one such birth occurs in a thousand hospitalised births, it is hardly necessary to open the flood- gates of euthanasia to deal with them.

One of the commonest defects for which euthanasia is used is spina bifida. This may involve mental retardation, will include many physical disabilities, and will need much surgery. But it is possible for many of them to survive the early difficulties and live with some handicaps. The hydrocephaly that often occurs can now be controlled, and large advances in treatment have been made in recent years. Doctors are sharply divided about whether this condition should be managed by "benign neglect" or not.

Under the older medical ethics of the Hippocratic oath, gravely defective infants were treated, like other patients, according to a policy of medical indications alone. They were helped if it was possible. If treatment could not help their condition, they were made comfortable and allowed, but not forced, to die. They were not starved to death for their own sake, or for that of parents or medical staff.

Particularly in this third kind of euthanasia it is perfectly apparent that the sacred restraints which once protected the life of the weak and the unwanted have now substantially broken down. As the American theologian Paul Ramsey has written: "Future historians may record that it was over the dead bodies of our children that euthanasia first came to be accepted in our society." There has been no strong or consistent opposition from the Christian churches. Indeed the Anglican church of Canada has produced a book which makes a principle of refusing to condemn the principle of euthanasia.

II

In the confines of this writing we are simply going to point to various changes in the application of certain key words and phrases, by which popular language has helped to cover up what has been happening to our society's perception of human life. This language, by its familiarity and ambiguity, can bind together the religious believer and the atheist, people who hold very different beliefs as to the nature of things. It is not surprising that the softening up for "mercy killing" and "people selection" should be done by slogans and language changes, since the public view of abortion has already been turned upside down by the same process. The words we are going to examine are: "person", "personhood" and "humanhood", "death with dignity", and "quality of life".

The first group of words to be examined is "person", "personhood", and "humanhood". Without the new distinctions that have accrued to "person", it would have been very unlikely that believers and atheists could speak the same language about euthanasia.

For many centuries, the most general meaning of the word "person" has been that of individual man, woman or child, as distinct from a non-human animal. From being mainly a neutral word, its meaning has gradually become more precise and more positive, through association with its use in law and the language of democracy. It suggests now an acknowledgement of respect for another member of our species, to whom we grant the same uniqueness and the same rights that we claim for ourselves. Among Christians, "person" has been given still weightier associations by its application in a special sense to the Trinity. Except for the Divine Trinity, all other persons are human beings, and until very recently all human beings were persons. As the idea of soul was made opaque under the influence of modern science, "person" was brought in to maintain the dignity of the individual. In the famous *Roe v. Wade* decision in 1973, the American Supreme Court decided that foetuses were not "persons in the full sense". The concept was still applied to all born human offspring. But in the last years of the 1970s, discrimination between persons and non-persons has become common among doctors, lawyers and theologians. Already the decision of which infants to save and which to neglect is not made on medical considerations alone but according to which is judged a person.

In 1972 Joseph Fletcher, once an Episcopalian clergyman, proposed fifteen indicators of what he called "humanhood". These indicators have had great influence on this continent. Among them he singled out above all "neocortical function"—that is, the functioning of that part of the brain from which come our intellectual activities. He assumed that these activities can be measured by a person's ability with I.Q. tests. Thus he writes: "Any individual of the species homo sapiens who falls below the I.Q. 40 mark in a Stanford-Binet test....is questionably a person; below the 20 mark, not a person."[1]

Fletcher applies this proposition with shocking consistency. Anybody who has knowledge of the retarded knows that children with Down's syndrome are usually capable of wonderful powers of affection and communication. Yet Fletcher makes quite clear what he would do with them. "True guilt," he writes "arises only from an offense against a person, and a Down's is not a person."[2] (Notice that the title of the article is "The Right to Die," when he is in this case talking of the right to kill.) In other words, it is quite proper to kill the baby at birth.

Fletcher's indicator is appalling because it identifies our humanity with our intellect. Traditional teaching has always praised intellectual activity, but it has also known that it is subordinate to love and must be used in the service of love. We all know people less clever than ourselves who are much finer persons than we are. On the other hand, anybody who works in a university knows cleverer people than himself who are mean and small-minded. Are we saying that the image of God in the soul depends above all on how well we can think? What then becomes of the account of God as love? And clearly the implication is present in Fletcher's indicators: if the right to claim personhood depends on the degree of our brain power, then we must conclude that the higher the I.Q. the more perfect the person. What then becomes of St. Paul's great thirteenth chapter of First Corinthians?

To exalt neo-cortical function says something very strange about God's love for us. As Paul Ramsey writes: "There is no indication at all that God is a rationalist whose care is a function of indicators of our personhood, or of our achievement within those capacities."[3] Moreover God's presence in and for someone else is certainly not dependent on our recognition of it. Surely we cannot tell how God communicates with those who do not make it on the Stanford-Binet test. At this point, agnosticism is the appropriate response.

The exaltation of the intellectual activities goes with the phrase "mere biological life". This is an expression which should make us cautious. As a phrase it is almost meaningless, as every living body is the body of a particular being, in this case an imperfect human being.

This identification of cleverness with "personhood" must also have obvious social implications in terms of the era we are living in. It should not be forgotten that the country which had the highest rate of literacy and the most advanced educational system in the world was Germany. Yet Germany produced the Hitlerian regime of total war and genocide. Indeed euthanasia was carried out because of the belief that certain human beings were "non-persons". As a very great German, Luther, once said, a nation which educates itself without love will become a nation of clever devils. Faith is the experience that the intellect is illuminated by love.

What does it portend for the future that the distinction should be made between human beings who are to be called persons and those who are not? If the soul can be measured and its value to God determined by an I.Q. test, does this not give society the right to rid itself not only of the retarded, but also of the useless aged? From there is a small step to the permanently ill and then beyond that to the non-conformists and beyond that to the politically dissident. Indeed it is just because Christianity proclaims the God who is love that we are asked to be tender to those persons who find it hard to realise their full personhood. Clever technocrats who have dropped their religious beliefs may decide that if you have not reached such and such an intellectual level, then you are not to be counted as a person. But Christians cannot so decide, because we were called to love our neighbours and not just the neighbours who are qualified on the Stanford-Binet test.

The second phrase to be considered is "death with dignity". The prospect of death can be unacceptable to all our instincts, the end of our "little brief authority"; dignity is one of the beautiful rewards of being human. No wonder the slogan "death with dignity" is irresistible. The very concept overcomes one of the horrors in our anticipation of our own death. We want it for ourselves, how can we deny it to others if it is in our power to give it to them?

Two main questions arise: can dignity be integral to human death? If so, what kind of dignity will it be?

The meaning of the word "dignity" is near to "worthiness", often the visible expression of the inner strength and worthiness that calls for respect in others. In so far as "dignity" means being in command of oneself and one's bodily functions, independent of the help of others, free from medical intervention, showing neither fear nor pain, it is irreconcilable with most kinds of dying and with all kinds of death. If that were an adequate account of human dignity, the death of Socrates would be more dignified than the death of Christ, and a well planned suicide better than either. This must be the kind of dignity that the leader of "Exit" referred to when he declared that suicide and voluntary euthanasia were the only ways to die with dignity.

Most of us have forgotten our true status. We do not have complete control of ourselves, we are not independent of others, at birth and death we are helpless, and never at any time are we autonomous (the maker of our own laws). In much modern theology about death, it seems to have been forgotten that we are creatures, dependent on God's love, and not simply our own masters. Autonomy is far from Gethsemane, and man is never more supremely dignified than when he manages, with whatever agony, to say with Christ: "Not my will but Thine be done". This is surely the kind of dignity which St. Peter is promised by Christ: "When thou shalt be old, thou shalt stretch forth thy hands and another shall gird thee, and carry thee whither thou wouldst not." (*John* 21:18.) As G. K. Chesterton has said: "God alone knoweth the praise of death."

The third phrase to be considered is "quality of life". Nearly two hundred years ago Dr. Christophe Hufeland wrote: "If the physician presumes to take into consideration in his work whether a life has value or not, the consequences are boundless, and the physician becomes the most dangerous man in the state." In 1920 a book was published in Germany called *The Release of the Destruction of Life Devoid of Value,* by a prominent jurist, Karl Binding, and a distinguished psychiatrist, Alfred Hoche. It advocated that there should be no legal penalty for the killing of "absolutely worthless human beings". It sold well and was very influential. It paved the way for the later activities of the Nazis.

Today the idea of life devoid of value is very ordinary. It is usually expressed by the innocent sounding phrase, "quality of life". When it is used positively, it suggests the caring professions, working together to improve living conditions for the less fortunate. As a slogan it is similar to "every child a wanted child". The phrases sound pleasant but they hide their own main point: what is going to happen to those not considered to have quality of life? It is a sad fact that in the context of medical and life-and-death decisions, quality of life becomes relevant mainly when used negatively. When a patient is normal and the means of helping him available, he will be given the indicated treatment as part of ordinary medical practice, without any reference to "quality of life" decisions. When a patient is abnormal, "quality of life" arises in consideration of whether his life is worth preserving.

Of course, if quality of life criteria are used negatively for stopping life support for a dying patient, no killing is being done. To repeat, letting the dying die is not euthanasia. Hippocrates put the matter well: "In general terms, [medicine] is to do away with the suffering of the sick, to lessen the violence of their diseases, and to refuse to treat those who are overmastered by their diseases, realising that in such cases medicine is powerless."

Nevertheless the fact that "quality of life" statements are frequently heard in innocent if unnecessary contexts makes the phrase all the more acceptable when it is sounding someone's death knell. Should life-saving surgery be done on an infant whose intelligence will be lower than normal (as in Down's syndrome babies with atresia)? Should an elderly patient be refused help because his or her clarity is starting to disappear? Should unborn infants be aborted when amniocentesis shows abnormalities which will seriously lower their quality of life? Judgements so based can be applied more and more widely. Life-saving treatment can be refused to the retarded, just because they are retarded.

Decisions for euthanasia based on "quality of life" assume that we are in a position to judge when someone else's life is not worth living. There is abolutely no evidence that the handicapped or the retarded would prefer to be dead. How do we compare an imperfect or restricted life with no life at all? Suicide among the handicapped is lower than among "normal" people. Can we assume that other people would prefer death if they were smart enough to realise how wretched their lives were compared to "normal" people? This argument is often put forward quite seriously.

"Quality of life" has a persuasive ring about it. To repeat, we all want a good life. But where do the implications of the slogan lead? When it is used so as to imply that some people have the right to judge that others do not have the right to be, then its political implications lead straight to totalitarianism. It must be remembered that "quality of life" was made central to political thought by the philosopher Nietzsche, who taught the sacred right of "merciless extinction" of large masses of men.

The three ideas which have been discussed — "death with dignity" and human automony, the distinction between "persons" and "non-persons", and "quality of life" judgements — all have something in common. They are all used dogmatically, leading to great confidence in our right to control human life. These are areas where the great religious tradition at its best has been restrained by agnosticism and a sense of transcendent mystery. Some believers have tried to combine these two views of life in a crudely simplistic manner. They have identified the freedoms technology gives us with the freedom given by truth. The result in the public world, if policy flowed from this identification, would be the destruction of cherished political freedoms.

Abortion and Rights

with Sheila Grant

I

We are often told these days that the rights of women
require the freedom to obtain abortions as part of the
liberty and privacy proper to every individual. When the
argument for easy abortion is made on the basis of rights, it
clearly rests on the weighing of the rights of some against
the rights of others. The right of a woman to have an
abortion can only be made law by denying to another
member of our species the right to exist. The right of
women to freedom, privacy and other good things is put
higher than the right of the foetus to continued existence.

Behind this conflict of rights, there is unveiled in the
debate about abortion an even more fundamental question
about rights themselves. What is it about human beings

that makes it proper that we should have any rights at all? Because of this the abortion issue involves all modern societies in basic questions of political principle.

These questions of principle were brought out into the open for Americans, when the Supreme Court of that country made it law that no legislation can be passed which prevents women from receiving abortions during the first six months of pregnancy. In laying down the reasons for that decision, the judges speak as if they were basing it on the supremacy of rights in a democratic society. But to settle the case in terms of rights, the judges say that the mother has all the rights, and that the foetus has none. Because they make this distinction, the very principle of rights is made dubious in the following way. In negating all rights to the foetuses, the court says something negative about what they are, namely that they are such as to warrant no right to continued existence. And because the foetus is of the same species as the mother, we are inevitably turned back onto the fundamental question of principle: what is it about the mother (or any human being) that makes it proper that she should have rights? Because in the laws about abortion one is forced back to the stark comparison between the rights of members of the same species (our own), the foundations of the principles behind rights are unveiled inescapably. What is it about our species that gives us rights beyond those of dogs or cattle?

The legal and political system, which was the noblest achievement of the English-speaking societies, came forth from our long tradition of free institutions and Common Law, which was itself produced and sustained by centuries of Christian belief. Ruthlessness in law and politics was limited by a system of legal and political rights which guarded the individual from the abuses of arbitrary power, both by the state and other individuals. The building of this system has depended on the struggle and courage of many, and was fundamentally founded on the Biblical assumption that human beings are the children of God. For this reason, everybody should be properly protected by carefully defined rights. Those who advocate easy abortion in the name of rights are at the same time unwittingly undermining the very basis of rights. Their complete disregard for the rights of the unborn weakens the very idea of rights itself. This weakening does not portend well for the continuing health of our system.

In the modern era, terrible programmes of persecution have been carried out by regimes of almost every persuasion, not only against political opponents, but against whole races and against whole classes of people, such as the aged and the unprotected young. Where the doctrine of rights has been denied (above all the right to existence), whole groups of individuals have been left completely unprotected. Mass murder comes when we forget what a human being is, and begin to regard people as accidental conglomerations of matter. A technological vision of man or woman as an object means that we can apply our 'improvements' to them as objects with increasing efficiency. Once we deny justice to any human life, then we are well on the road to the kind of thinking that impels a fascist dictatorship to the horrors of the death camp and the purge.

Our century's tragic record of man's inhumanity to his own kind makes especially frightening the argument that the foetus in the womb has no rights. The talk about rights by those who work for abortion on demand has a sinister tone to it, because in it is implied a view of human beings which destroys any reason why any of us should have rights. What will be demanded next: the denial of the rights of the aged, the mentally retarded and the insane, the denial of the rights of the less economically privileged who cannot defend themselves? Our system of legal and political rights is the crown of our heritage, and it is being undermined. The denial of any right to existence for the foetus has already been declared officially in the United States.

II

The validity of this argument must stand or fall primarily on the assertion that the foetus is a living member of our species. It is a fact, accepted by all scientists, that the individual has his or her unique genetic code from conception onwards. He or she is therefore not simply part of the mother's body. After 18 days a heart beats; at three and a half weeks, when the mother may not yet know she is pregnant, there are already the beginnings of eyes, spinal cord, nervous system, thyroid gland, lungs, stomach, liver, kidneys and intestines; at six weeks brain waves can be detected. It is not necessary to elaborate on the further development. It can be found in any textbook of embryology. It cannot therefore be denied by those favouring easy abortion. Even Doctor Morgentaler, the Canadian abortionist, justifies himself by asserting how very small the foetus is at early stages, as if size were an argument.

The scientific evidence cannot be denied; it is, however, ignored. It is at this point that there seems to be a complete breakdown of communication between those favouring easy abortion and those against it. The central reason for this impasse seems to be a confusion in the use of words to describe what the foetus is. This confusion is a playing with words, which often leads to wishful thinking as to what is being done in an abortion. Therefore it is necessary to look carefully at such words as 'human', 'human beings', 'person', and 'life'. What frequently happens is that the primary meanings of these words become lost, because they are overlaid by specific meanings.

For example, the usual name nowadays for a member of our species is 'human being'. In the Oxford Dictionary the word 'human' is defined first in the generic sense, 'of, or belonging to man', then later as 'having the qualities or attributes proper to a man'. This meaning was retained in the word 'humane', (the older spelling of 'human'), which now means 'characterised by such behaviour or disposition towards others as befits a man'. The generic sense of 'human', which covers all our species, is specialised into meanings which only apply to members of the race at their best. Words do not hold their meanings in water-tight compartments. We often, and rightly, use 'human' in such contexts as 'human values', 'inhuman cruelty', 'what properly befits a human being' or even 'a very human person', where the word means much more than 'belonging to the human race', and suggests the characteristics of men and women at their most mature.

Similarly, the word 'person' can mean an individual of our species; but can also connote a mature man or woman, capable of 'personal relationships'; 'personal integrity' etc. In these contexts it is almost identical with the specialised uses of 'human'. The Dred Scott Decision in 1856 by the American Supreme Court ruled that although Blacks were human beings, they were not 'persons' in the eyes of the law. The 14th Amendment to their constitution was enacted specifically to overturn this, and interpreted 'person' as including all living beings. So if, with vague 19th Century ideas of personal quality in mind, we return to the naming

of ourselves as 'human beings', we are then apparently able
to exclude the foetus from being thought of as human. We
may also have no difficulty in excluding other categories of
mankind that do not measure up to our view of what is
'truly human in the fullest and most meaningful sense'.

A confusion is also found in the use of the word 'life'.
'The foetus may be alive in a biological sense', we are told,
'but human, no'. It is implied that to talk of our species in
terms of biological life is to talk on a very low level indeed.
In fact 'biological life' is a misleading tautology. There is
no such thing in nature as a living organism that has
merely 'biological life'. It must belong to some species,
even if it is only an amoeba. If the foetus is alive, yet is not
human, what is it? No woman has yet given birth to a
cat—although the National Council of Women are evident-
ly not quite sure about this. In 1967, they presented a
resolution to a Parliamentary Committee in which abortion was defined as the "premature expulsion of the mam-
malian foetus." It is impossible to meet a mammal, pure
and simple. One meets a cat, or a dog, or a human being.
There is another kind of double-talk about life, which has a
place in the U.S. Supreme Court Decision, *Roe v. Wade*.
After viability (the date of which will vary according to the
sophistication of our current supportive techniques), a
foetus becomes legally recognisable as 'potential life'. Presumably 'potential' must mean 'capable of, but not yet
possessing'. By this vague phrase do they mean that the
foetus is not alive? If not alive, do they mean it is dead, or
what? Even the U.S. Supreme Court must know the difference between a living foetus and a dead one. There is no
halfway house. Beings with only 'potential' life do not suck
their thumbs in the womb in preparation for the breast. It
makes perfect sense to say that we are all potentially dead,
but it does not make sense to say that the foetus is 'potential
life'.

It is best to be suspicious of such phrases as 'potential life', 'person in the whole sense', 'human in the full sense of the word'. They confuse what is being done in abortion. How can the primary or plain sense of 'human' be denied to the foetus? What a dog begets is canine: what we beget is human.

III

In our day, the struggle for rights has often been effective. It now runs counter to the temper of our society to challenge the claims of personal freedom. Men and women are grasping towards an understanding which would preclude violence against one another. The noble attempt to eliminate capital punishment is a good example. Women are struggling courageously for their proper equality. What of children? In the preamble of the U.N.'s Declaration of the Rights of a Child (Nov. 29th, 1959), it is stated that the Declaration is necessary "because the child, by reason of his physical and mental immaturity, needs special safeguards and care, including legal protection before as well as after birth." It is ironic that at the time of these victories there has arisen a new category of the unprotected. Despite the tradition of rights in which we were nurtured, the unborn child in the United States has been deprived of the right to exist, and the pressure for this is mounting in Canada. Strangely enough, the unborn still have some rights: they can inherit under a will, they can even be recognised as plaintiffs in a law suit. But for the individuals who can be put to death at the will of the very person who brought them into existence, such rights as these are rather a bad joke.

Some distinctions must be made here between the legal situation in Canada and in the States. In January, 1973, the Supreme Court of the U.S. made its declaration in *Roe v. Wade*. It affirmed a new right, nowhere mentioned in their constitution but 'felt' to be 'intended'. No legislation can infringe the right of a woman to procure the termination of her pregnancy. For the first six or seven months, no reason at all need be given for the killing of the developing child. After that time, though still declared not to be a 'person in the whole sense' he or she is recognised as 'potential life'. After the sixth month of a foetus' life, some bureaucratic red tape is required before he or she can be killed; namely, one doctor must declare it necessary for the mother's health. This is understood as having its broadest interpretation, that of general 'well being'.

Canada's position is slightly different. More red tape is required. An abortion may be performed at any time during the pregnancy, on the recommendation of one doctor, which a committee of three doctors ratifies. The committee does not need to see the woman. The numbers of ratifications done in a short time are very large. A disinclination towards bearing a child is frequently interpreted as a danger to mental health. In some parts of Canada we already have *de facto* abortion on demand. In 1983, according to Statistics Canada, 61,800 legal abortions were performed, and the number increases each year, although medical necessities decrease. It is obvious that convenience, rather than danger, is already often the criterion. Yet there is pressure today for still easier laws. The only possible extension would be abortion on demand.

What has happened to our belief in rights, that in the name of a lesser right, the primary one, the right to life, can be denied to members of our own species? Not only is the woman's own right to life affirmed but it includes her right to freedom and privacy, and well-being, and all sorts of other good things. Yet she herself, her own unique unrepeatable self, was once growing in her mother's womb. What magic has occurred with the passage of time that gives her all these rights, and denies the foetus any?

There are, of course, events in which the rights can really be seen to conflict in equality of extremity. The tragic cases are where the deepest rights of two human beings conflict, where the choice is between two human lives, not merely between life and difficult circumstances. Girls who are made pregnant at a very early age may be open to extreme dangers both psychological and physical. Doctors may judge rightly that there are circumstances of rape where the foetus should not be allowed to survive. It seems quite clear to me that when the mother will die if there is no abortion, then the foetus should be aborted. This writing does not imply that there are no proper occasions for abortion. But from the statistics of the massive numbers on this continent, it is made plain that only a very small fraction of abortions are done out of medical necessity. What is at stake in the rare cases of proper abortion must be a conflict at the depths of the lives of two human beings—the possibility of survival.

Light can be thrown on this denial of rights by looking at a familiar quotation: "We hold these truths to be self-evident; that all men are created equal, that they are endowed by their Creator with inalienable rights, that among these rights are life....that to secure these rights, governments are instituted among men". Fine, ringing words, but alas, no longer self-evident. Our world has changed. Many believe that we are accidental beings in a world that came to be through chance. In such a situation the very foundations of the doctrine of rights have been eroded. All men are not created equal; they are not created at all. Justice can become a privilege society grants to some of its people, if they are the right age, and sufficiently like most other people. One can foresee a time when before one can qualify for rights a kind of Means Test may be used: 'Are you human in the fullest sense of the word?' 'Are you still enjoying the quality of life?' And here is the crunch; as the foetus loses out on this ethic, so will all the weak, the aged, the infirm, the unproductive. If we come to believe that we are not creatures, but accidents, rights will no longer be given in the very nature of our legal system. The most powerful among us will then decide who are to have rights and who are not.

The effect of this undermining of our political tradition is often sugar-coated by talk about 'quality of life'. The phrase 'quality of life' has a high-minded ring about it. Like the slogan, 'every child a wanted child', it is impossible to be against it. Of course it is better for children to be wanted rather than rejected, and for lives to have a high quality rather than a low one. But let us remember for what purpose these slogans are now mainly used. They are used negatively, and with terrible destructive implications. Every child should be a wanted child, so destroy those that do not seem to be wanted. It would seem that only 'quality of life' deserves our respect, not life itself. Of course, when 'quality of life' is urged for constructive purposes, it is indeed a compassionate approach to human suffering, but when we justify abortion for hedonistic reasons, with some lives down-graded as expendable, its proper use is perverted.

In case this account seems exaggerated, it is worth looking at the list of characteristics drawn up by the Episcopalian clergyman, Joseph Fletcher, by which life may be recognized as 'human'. The list includes 'self awareness', 'a sense of time', 'self control', 'capability of relating to others', 'the ability to communicate', 'a concern for others', 'control over existence', and 'a balance of rationality and feeling'. A bit unnerving, when one looks at oneself. How many of us would qualify? This is an example of the word 'human' being made qualitative and then identified with the generic sense. But one cannot really afford to laugh, as Fletcher has had enormous influence. It is no accident that he is also a member of the Board of Directors of the Euthanasia Education Council. His criteria for humanity work equally destructively at the beginning or the end of life.

Allied to the 'quality of life' concept is the phrase 'the accruing value of life', by which the United Church attempted to justify abortion (in *Abortion, A Study,* 1970). Exactly what value is supposed to be accruing is not very clear. Is it physical strength, intellectual development, self consciousness or what? Presumably this accruing quality becomes a declining one for those growing older and feebler. Are clever people more valuable than the rest of us—are the healthy more valuable than the crippled? Once we start grading the right to life in terms of quality, our criteria are seen to exclude more and more groups from human status. What will we be willing to do to these groups?

IV

The most pressing warning of how far the destruction of rights could go in the western world took place in Nazi Germany. We, in the English-speaking world, would like to think of this as a monstrous happening which was defeated, and stopped, and which has no relation to ourselves. But if we look at some of the basic programmes carried out by the Nazis toward their own people, we may find that whatever our revulsion, our society seems to be moving away from the clear principles which would condemn these practices.

The Nazi programme of euthanasia of the insane and the incurable was extended in 1943 to include children orphaned by the war. These children were put to death in the gas chambers along with the incurable and the insane. The country was thus relieved of the burden of those who could not care for themselves. The techniques of the gas chambers and the crematoria were used first for such people, then extended to the Jews, the gypsies and political opponents. Hitler had to keep these programmes of euthanasia against his own people as secret as possible. Largely through the courage of Bishop Galen, the programmes became known to the public, and evoked great horror among the German people, even though they were living in a totalitarian state.

We, of course, do not yet kill our mentally ill (except when we treat infants with 'benign neglect'). Nevertheless, we are moving towards ways of thought which could be used to justify such actions. Blacks and prisoners, the mentally ill and foetuses have more and more become the subjects of experiments. In none of these cases can 'informed consent' be a likely reality. The next extension of the denial of rights seems likely to be euthanasia for the aged. (What is meant here by euthanasia is deliberate killing, not the withdrawal by a doctor of extraordinary measures to prolong life in hopeless cases.) The euphemisms are ready: 'a good death', 'death with dignity', 'life without value', 'choosing of the moment', 'assisting nature', and best of all, perhaps, because it preserves the illusion of autonomy, 'suicide by proxy'. Another frightening one is 'providing for those who cannot speak for themselves'. What provisions might not be made, were this to become legal?

In our movement towards euthanasia, the altruistic principle, the desire to take life in order to spare suffering, is often mixed with more practical considerations about the cost and inconvenience of prolonging unproductive life. It will start, of course, with hard cases, and those desiring death, or unable to say whether they do or not. Let us remember the 1969 amendments to the Criminal Code on Abortion; what was intended by the law as provision for hard cases has quickly become provision for convenience. Our language is nearly ready for it, our vocabulary is well softened up. If a developing baby can be called (and thought of) as 'foetal tissue', and his or her violent death as 'termination of pregnancy', it is not fanciful to expect many more helpful euphemisms for getting rid of unwanted people. If this sounds alarmist, it is well to remember the figures of abortions since the law was amended in 1969. In 1970 there were 11,152 legal abortions in Canada; in 1983, 61,800, a figure which does not include those performed at the Morgentaler clinics. The situation is clearly self-accelerating. If women know they never need bear a child they have conceived, they are less and less likely to face the initial inconveniences. We have moved fast in a few years toward the point where, in the name of convenience, we say that a woman has an absolute right to an abortion and an unborn child has no right to existence.

As we move into the apogee of technological civilisation, nobody can predict what it is going to be like in every detail. We can expect, however, that technology will be more and more focussed upon cybernetics, the art of the steersman, and will be even more intricately connected with the overall direction of society. Will abortion simply become an instrument of cybernetics?

Of course, abortion is not only a public, but a private matter—a question which individuals have to face in the agony of their own lives. About such private matters, writers must remember always that people do their own living as they do their own dying. It is difficult enough to look after one's own anguishes. Writers can speak generally about what is being done in an act such as abortion: they cannot judge how others cope with the awful responsibilities of time. And yet the public place we give abortion will be a central mark by which it can be known what rights will be given to the weak by our directors. Obviously the justice of a society is well defined in terms of how it treats the weak. And there is nothing human which is weaker than the foetus.

Notes

Thinking About Technology

1 The extension in the conception of machine may tend to put in question the commonsense idea of the machine as instrument. This fuller conception in computers draws closer the analogy between machines and brains. Without raising the present technical dispute about the relative capacities of the human brain and computers, and also without trespassing on the proper realm of science fiction, it is easy to speculate on a development of machines which would bring the analogy still closer. A synonym for a machine is a 'contrivance'. There was once a verb in popular usage 'to machine' which meant the same as 'to contrive'. These potential machines of the future, if their powers were more nearly identical to the human brain, would indeed be human contrivances, but would they be human instruments?

Nietzsche and the Ancients

1 See *Studies in Nietzsche and the Classical Tradition*, the University of North Carolina Press, 1976, pp. 1-15.

2 Heidegger's *Nietzsche* is surely a *sine qua non* for anybody who would understand Nietzsche. Commentaries of one great thinker on another are so rare that they should never be neglected.

3 Letter to Brandes 1888.

4 An even more complacent book in the same tradition is Sir Kenneth Dover's recent *Greek Homosexuality*. The book's coziness flattens out all the complexities of that subject.

5 See J.A. Doull "Quebec Independence and an Independent Canada", paper in *Modernity and Responsibility*, ed. E. Combs, University of Toronto Press, 1983.

6 *Nietzsche Werke,* Naumann, Leipzig, 1904, XIV, p. 385. This translation and the ones that follow are my poor own. How does one translate properly this polysyllabic language of compounds into a language which has reached its greatest heights in the use of the monosyllable? How does one not lose both the substance and the rhetoric of that immoderate stylist?

7 Nietzsche, *op. cit. Nachgelassene Fragmente* 1844.

Faith and the Multiversity

1 S. Weil "La Pesanteur et La Grace" Plon, Paris, 1948. My translation. The greater the writer the more hesitant is the translator.

2 Please see here the relation of what is said in the text to the Appendix at the end.

3 The tendency of human beings to become self-engrossed has been encouraged in our era, because the distinctiveness of modern political thought has been the discovery of 'individuality.' It is not my purpose here to discuss the good or evil of that 'discovery' but simply to state that one of its consequences has been to legitimize concentration on the self.

4 *Mozart's Briefe,* ed. L. Nohl, 2nd edition, pp. 443-444. It is significant that in quoting this passage Heidegger stops before Mozart's words about the best gift of God. (See *Der Satz vom Grund,* Pfullingen 1957, chapter 9.) Indeed in his comments on this quotation Heidegger writes of Mozart as "the lute of God"—a metaphor he takes from a poem of Angelus Silesius. But is Mozart's account of his activity properly grasped in calling him "the lute of God"? To put the matter directly, was there not some moment when Mozart could have exercised the liberty of indifference to what had been given him? On the one hand Kant's insistence on our own autonomy kills a proper partaking in beauty and in its

extremity leads to the modern doctrine of art as human creativity (whatever that may mean) and so art is understood quite apart from the divine gift. But on the other hand the metaphor of "the lute of God" about Mozart sweeps away the liberty of indifference which is what we properly mean by freedom, in this case the freedom of the artist. At the height of sanctity Angelus Silesius' metaphor might be appropriate. But Heidegger uses it here about an artist, albeit a supreme one. There has been some questioning of the authenticity of this passage from Mozart's letters, but in 1957 Heidegger says it is authentic.

5 It is neither my business here, nor would it be my competence, to write of the development of truth about evolution since Darwin; *e.g.,* to discuss the correct way of thinking about the units of selection.

6 *The Will to Power,* no. 822. If this writing was first concerned with the history of thought it would be interesting to trace the similarities and differences between Nietzsche's words and Bacon's vulgar patronising of poetry in the second book of *The Advancement of Learning.* It was the fate of English thought to understand the early outlines of technological society; it was the fate of German thought later to look its deeper consequences in the face. When we read Matthew Arnold's comfortable phrases about art taking the place of religion, one should compare them with Nietzsche's unflinching recognition of the consequences of the disjunction between beauty and truth.

7 As an example, a great agony arises today among Christians who wish to be doctors. They find it difficult to be admitted for such training unless they are willing to take part in the full work of their teachers. As the full work requires that they take part in a steady programme of foeticide (in a majority of cases simply undertaken for convenience), they are not in a position to gain admission to that training. That exclusion is naturally not much publicised by the medical profession. But such practical dilemmas are not my concern here, except to say again, "matter is our infallible judge".

Acknowledgements

We would like to thank the following for their kind permission to reprint some of the essays which appeared in earlier versions in other volumes:

"Nietzsche and the Ancients: Philosophy and Scholarship", *Dionysius*, vol. III, December 1979, pp. 5-16.

"Research in the Humanities". This essay was originally published in John Woods and Harold G. Coward, editors, *Humanities in the Present Day* (Waterloo: Wilfrid Laurier University Press, 1979).

"Euthanasia", from *Care for the Dying and Bereaved*, I. Gentles, ed. (Toronto: The Anglican Book Centre, 1976).

"Abortion", from *The Right to Birth*, E. Fairweather and I. Gentles, eds. (Toronto: The Anglican Book Centre, 1976).

Other books from Anansi Press which you may find of interest. Available through your local bookseller, or please write to us for further information.

Books by or about George Grant:
George Grant, *Technology and Empire: Perspective on North America*
George Grant, *English-Speaking Justice*
Larry Schmidt, editor, *George Grant in Process: Essays and Conversations*

Biography:
Charles Taylor, *Radical Tories: The Conservative Tradition in Canada*
Charles Taylor, *Six Journeys: A Canadian Pattern*
Marian Fowler, *The Embroidered Tent: Five Gentlewomen in Early Canada*

Interviews:
Graeme Gibson, *Eleven Canadian Novelists*
Bruce Meyer & Brian O'Riordan, *In Their Words: Interviews with Fourteen Canadian Writers*
Donald Smith, *Voices of Deliverance: Interviews with Quebec and Acadian Writers*

Literary Criticism:
Margaret Atwood: *Second Words: Essays in Criticism*
Margaret Atwood: *Survival: A Thematic Guide to Canadian Literature*
Northrop Frye: *The Bush Garden: Essays on the Canadian Imagination*
Northrop Frye: *Divisions on a Ground: Essays on Canadian Culture*